Life's ~~Too Short for Leftovers~~

"Michael Ditchfield's new book is a must-read for anyone interested in changing the world for the better. *Life's Too Short for Leftovers* demystifies how to make positive, sustainable and lasting change in communities around the world.

With a focus on Africa, Michael reminds us that we cannot ignore the needs of that continent and the tremendous history, hope, talent and opportunity that exist there. Michael challenges people and institutions to step up, showcasing the interdependency of all communities.

As someone who has been working on these issues for the past twenty years, I am inspired by this well-written book and Michael's personal efforts in Africa and beyond. A must read."

—Patrick Gaston, President,
Western Union Foundation

"Chef and humanitarian Michael Ditchfield shares the lessons he has learned from his greatest teachers in life. These voices—full of hard-won wisdom from the people of Ethiopia, Rwanda, the Sudan, and more—make *Life's Too Short for Leftovers* well worth reading. Inspirational!"

—Dawn Engle, Co-Founder, PeaceJam
Six-time Nominee for the Nobel Peace Prize

"A fascinating journey through the places we've heard about but may never visit—where we send money with little effect, and where our help is still desperately needed. An inspiring recipe for changing the world."
—Ryan Scott, CEO and Founder, Causecast

"Michael's book will transform people's lives. For those in bondage, it will liberate you. For those who need to be released from anger and resentment, Michael has answers for you. I recommend *Life's Too Short for Leftovers* for anyone who wants to know more, take action, and enjoy life.
—Jean-Paul Samputu, World Renowned Musician and Peace Activist. Winner of the Kora (African Grammy)

"Michael is a rare human being. Not only does he possess a kind compassionate spirit—and is always ready for adventure—but he is also able to write about his wide and varied experience in a witty and engaging voice that draws the reader in and delivers remarkable insight for us all."
—Henry Ansbacher, Oscar- and Emmy-nominated Film Director

"Ditchfield shines...the book will inspire readers to want to do their part to become better citizens of the world."
—*Blue Ink Review*

"Ditchfield offers unique and inspirational ideas to act on as we connect with others around this world."

—Suzanne Brown, *Denver Post*

"From devastated countryside to comfortable kitchens, the author relates his encounters in clear, confident prose and carefully balances hard facts and statistics about emerging nations with playful observations and hopeful good humor... A series of moving, important stories from a passionate humanitarian..."

—*Kirkus Reviews*

"...there is no doubt that his book will leave loving fingerprints on many lives."

—Marta Gabre-Tsadick, CEO Project Mercy

Life's Too Short for Leftovers

9 Lessons from a Third World Kitchen

Michael Ditchfield

Black Crown Publishing
London

Life's Too Short for Leftovers:
9 Lessons from a Third World Kitchen
Published by Black Crown Publishing

Library of Congress Control Number: 2015937584
Ditchfield, Michael, Author
Life's Too Short for Leftovers:
9 Lessons from a Third World Kitchen
Michael Ditchfield

ISBN: 978-0-9962537-0-3

COOKING / Essays & Narratives
SOCIAL SCIENCE / Philanthropy & Charity

QUANTITY PURCHASES: Schools, companies, professional groups,
clubs, and other organizations may qualify for special terms
when ordering quantities of this title. For information, email
info@BlackCrownPublishing.com.

London

Printed in Canada

To the unknown—but not forgotten—
Ethiopian parking lot attendant

Angela,
Be yourself...
Everyone else is
taken!

INGREDIENTS

FOREWORD

by Doug Wead
New York Times bestselling author,
advisor to two presidents, presidential historian

Having spent time in Africa, my firsthand account of the continent is that we need to listen more, learn more, and act accordingly—especially where human lives are at stake. To that end, Michael Ditchfield champions greater awareness and understanding, and what it means to achieve a level playing field.

I first met Michael years ago at a charity dinner in Washington, D.C., with then-President Ronald Reagan. Even among the dignitaries and celebrities in attendance—from politicians to entertainers to sports figures—Michael's conviction and commitment to empower the powerless shone like a beacon.

Michael brought back from his experiences in Africa some valuable lessons that transform lives—ours and the lives of those whom we aim to serve and inspire. A deft storyteller, Michael shares his own journey with us, including his experiences with the people of Ethiopia, Rwanda, and Sudan. Along the way, we befriend him—sometimes through laughter, sometimes through tears, and always with new insight. We gain compassion for ourselves and others, and we come to admire the cast of everyday heroes introduced in these pages.

Michael feels strongly that we must contribute to the world as seen through the lens of moral responsibility. That's a timely message in a world where examples of the gap between the haves and the have-nots—and the gulf between peace and conflict— abound. He has devoted the rest of his life to lending a hand up in some of Africa's most troubled regions, and I applaud his efforts.

Life's Too Short for Leftovers is a compelling blueprint for transforming lives—starting with our own, and reaching beyond borders and across continents. There's much we can learn from lives seemingly different—and far more difficult—than ours. And there's much we can offer, no matter who we are. In this book, Michael guides the way from introspection to interconnectedness and ultimately, to love.

PREFACE

The Invitation

To upset a chef before you have taken the first bite of one of his signature dishes is not the smartest move ... especially if he's an Irish chef with a temper as hot as the stove on which he cooks.

I had ventured into Chef Noel Cunningham's upscale Denver restaurant, intending to enjoy a quiet evening filled with laughter and great food. I never envisioned that I would leave with something that would alter the course of my life. The way he emerged from the kitchen that Saturday evening and approached my table—a ladle in hand, flour covering his face, with a bowl of the same flour cradled under his arm—still makes me smile. "How much thicker do you want it?" were the first words I ever heard him mutter. His slight trace of an Irish accent brought my world to a standstill. I was dining with the enemy. Or so I thought at the time.

You see, I am English and have never really figured out the men in green. I don't believe it has anything to do with jealousy of their alleged culinary prowess or the fact that they imitate Scots by wearing kilts, claiming they are really aprons. As I see it, the Irish don't have a particularly adventurous sense of cooking—unless of course you count the hundred or so ways to boil a potato. This in itself laid out the battleground for our first exchange of verbal blows.

To this day, I maintain that the saffron sauce was much too thin. He maintained that I complained too much and that his only regret in life was allowing me into his restaurant. The hostess who took the reservation that evening is still looking for work. But we got through our rocky start and developed a profoundly meaningful friendship. From the moment I locked horns with this shy, hunched-over Irishman with salt-and-pepper hair, who seemed to carry the weight of the world on his shoulders, my life has never been the same.

I upset him that night, and I'm glad I did. It was the beginning of bringing the world a little closer together, one impoverished child at a time. We just didn't know it then.

INTRODUCTION

The Toast

"The price of greatness is responsibility."
~Winston S. Churchill

The recipe book for life can't be found in any library or bookstore. For each one of us, it's being written every day in response to our appetite for good, truth, and justice; and in response to a hunger more acute than the one we feel in our bellies. For some, it's a hunger of the heart to help others, especially children who are hurting, and to help bring peace to places where people live in fear.

When the game of soccer led me to America back in the 1980s, I didn't know that I would end up bringing sportsmanship to children in war-torn Africa. I never imagined that a dinner reservation in 1992 at a great restaurant in Denver, Colorado, would eventually connect me to a life mentor who would guide me to Ethiopia—and to the delights of cooking.

And I surely didn't know that in the kitchens and homes of the people of Ethiopia, Rwanda, and Sudan, I would find the common ground, the shared language, and the mutual values that would inspire me to help bring about change and deliver hope to developing countries in Africa ... and to play a part in making the world a safer and better place to live.

Noel Cunningham was one of the kindest, most gentle human beings you could ever hope to meet— a decent man known as Chef, although he maintained he was merely a cook. I, on the other hand, was under the impression that I knew it all—with little thought, let alone understanding, for what was happening outside my own egotistical bubble built around a soul in need of searching.

Noel cooked for the Beatles, Sheryl Crow, the Kennedys, and members of the Rolling Stones. He broke bread with the former prime minister of Canada, and even served lunch—under the watchful eye of the U.S. Secret Service—to the president of Rwanda.

He also made lunch in his restaurant with Morgan, a five-year-old girl suffering from leukemia who visited him at the restaurant every time she came for chemotherapy at a nearby hospital. When she died in 1998, Noel never really recovered. Her picture was a fixture in his cluttered office of accolades, which, for him, paled in comparison to the angelic smile that greeted him every day and lifted his spirits. He continued his quest for saving children with the same consistency that had, for years, been the hallmark of his cooking. Noel was giving before it was cool to give.

I haven't cooked for anyone noteworthy. To be honest, I haven't really cooked for anyone. The proof of my pudding is not in the eating, but in my refrigerator where nothingness is punctuated with a bottle of 1998 Dom Perignon and five bottles of Zino Davidoff cologne. I was content with living life happily shallow after.

Why would one of the greatest chefs in the world choose to help some of its poorest people? "Because," said Noel, "they say thank you." He was hard around the edges, but soft inside. He couldn't even pat himself on the back because of his stooped shoulders. Instead, others did it for him ... but it made him uncomfortable. He was a modest man.

When I lingered in his kitchen for any length of time, not only did I discover that he was one of the finest chefs ever to hold a knife, but that there was so much more to learn from him than the ingredients and preparation of a meal. A recipe for life was his specialty. Whether by watching him dice an onion dry-eyed or seeing him embrace an AIDS-infected child in Ethiopia with real, pained tears, I began to understand that what life sets out for you on your table is all there is.

Diced onions on a chopping block will be just that unless you combine them with other ingredients. The embrace of a child will be just that unless you offer that child more than a fleeting moment of physical presence. Noel was there to serve food and serve others. He had a firm grasp in the kitchen and a gentle hand in the world.

The Menu

*"No snowflake in an avalanche ever
feels responsible."*
~Stanisław Jerzy Lec

I couldn't think of a better place than Noel's restaurant to be simultaneously humbled and well-fed. He always made room for me after the lunch crowd had left. We sat together and drank tea with way too much milk and sugar (after all, the Irish have little taste when it comes to taste).

"What have you done for the world today?" he would ask. He wanted to know if I had done my homework, and I usually fumbled through a response that didn't merit his approval. He was relentless.

Once, I raised enough money to send soccer uniforms to Ethiopia. He did offer a thank-you—and coming from Chef that was probably the highest compliment one could hope for. *Finally*, I thought, *I have done my part.* I had secured the uniforms and Project Mercy had received them. Now I could get on with my life—a life that, upon reflection, only scratched the scratch on the scratch of the surface. But that initial feeling of accomplishment was similar to a feel-good massage. It was fleeting.

Eventually I booked a flight to Ethiopia to see first-hand what human survival was really about. Chef, too, made the trip (he actually booked it for me, carrying me through my partly guilt-ridden and partly petrified state). And so it was that Chef's kitchen of wisdom moved from his Denver restaurant to a converted cow barn in Ethiopia, where Marta Gabre-Tsadick and her husband, Demeke Tekle-Wold, have created an oasis of hope—Project Mercy—in the middle of a Godforsaken, drought-stricken land.

This was the kitchen of hope, where the former personal cook to the late Emperor Haile Selassie prepared breakfast and lunch for more than 1,000 children, the majority of whom walked barefoot for two hours to school every day for merely a chance to learn and dream. AIDS-ridden and devastated by famine, the country they had been born to was a wasteland inhabited by the walking dead. And yet, here—in the midst of all of such despair—hope had sprung eternal. The greatest blueprint for survival and self-sufficiency in the not-so-free world was right beneath my feet. Experiencing my first African sunrise, sitting beside my wise, yet soft-spoken, mentor, gave me purpose where before there had been none. Noel had brought me to the crossroads in my life.

The one place that brings people together—where they congregate and communicate—is the kitchen. But the kitchen of life in the Third World is like none other. It brought me a sense of empowerment that Chef had attempted to get across to me in his own kitchen. I was finally getting it: any kitchen in the world can bring about conflict, just as it can bring about harmony and resolution.

Whether we're talking about sports, politics, or religion over a pot of chili cooking here in the United States, or discussing where the next meal will come from over an open fire in a village in Ethiopia, or living in terror in a village in Darfur, wondering whether the devil will appear on horseback to slaughter mothers and children—there's much to consider and despair in our world. This realization of our collective suffering changed me.

It was a change that began the moment our Land Rover challenged Ethiopia's Rift Valley on the four-hour trek to Yetabon, along the way crossing paths with villagers—survivalists whose smiles were distorted by the few teeth they had left, and who had nothing except life itself. We gained momentum as we pulled up to Project Mercy where one hundred children—wearing the very same uniforms that I had sent over—greeted us in song. I was swept away the moment an HIV-afflicted child with nowhere left to turn sat on my lap outside the feeding center—his hollow eyes looking up toward heaven as mine looked down toward a hell.

Back in the United States, my changing spirit catapulted me forward on a rainy Sunday evening as I handed my parking ticket to an Ethiopian parking lot attendant to whom I dedicate this book. Recognizing my face from the documentary about our trip that had aired the previous week, he said something that I had never heard before and will never hear in quite the same way again:

"Thank you for saving my people."

It was then that I finally got it. The impact of his words launched me on a journey of my own. It compelled me to step up my involvement in the Third World and forge a new identity for myself that would forever be my measuring stick as a steward of this good earth.

It led to my working in Rwanda with some of the 95,000 children orphaned by the 1994 genocide (according to UNICEF), an atrocity that resulted in close to one million deaths in one hundred days. Imagine three 9/11s every day for one hundred days.

If only apathy could have been put on the back burner when Lieutenant-General Roméo Dallaire sent a cable on January 11, 1994 to UN Department of Peacekeeping Operations in New York. Dallaire, commander of UN forces at the time of the genocide, signed the cable, "Let's go." Dallaire was three months ahead of this preventable barbarity to which we contributed through detachment. Yet the UN rebuked him for exceeding his mandate. Common sense was anything but common.

When I arrived in Rwanda, however, I witnessed the results of hope and perseverance that had grown out of our collective neglect and indifference. I saw the beginnings of a brighter future. Restoring and maintaining peace was at the forefront, because the children of the Rwandan genocide were at an age where they could begin to comprehend what had happened.

From Rwanda, my trek took me to Sudan where I met the devil. He wasn't hard to find in this hellhole, which he furnished with corpses of the innocent. You only had to look into the eyes of the women who had been raped and tortured to see that he'd been here in all his infamy.

In Ethiopia it's self-sufficiency. In Rwanda it's self-dignity. In Sudan it's survival. The children of Ethiopia can smile when they have full stomachs. In Rwanda, it's harder to smile when you've witnessed the murder and rape of family and friends. In Sudan, there was nothing to smile about.

~

The horrors of 1994 must not be repeated. Indeed, we live in a world of second chances. We shouldn't ignore them—ignorance has already shown its ugly face and left a lasting impression—if only for the taste of a meal whose main ingredients of peace and decency last far longer than any expiration date.

In *The White Man's Burden*, author William Easterly puts into perspective an understanding of why money raised for Third World causes doesn't always reach the people it's intended for—the West has spent more than $2.3 trillion on foreign aid over the last fifty-five years, and yet children still go without twelve-cent medication. The film, *Poverty, Inc.*, further illuminates the challenges (and dismal failures) of poverty alleviation in developing countries. Alternately, on July 16, 2005, the sixth volume of the "Harry Potter" book series was delivered to nine million people in America and Britain. If only the Third World could have one day like that—substituting much-needed food and medicine deliveries.

After traveling to Rwanda, I realized that the miles seem much shorter when lives are to be saved. Indeed, we will never accomplish everything that we have dreamed, but we will accomplish nothing that we haven't dreamed. But now that I'm awake to the needs of emerging nations, I will never again allow myself a day in which I do not attempt to dream and make a difference. The dream continued when I had the opportunity to return one of the first Lost Boys of Sudan to his village. It was there that I saw firsthand the devastation that has torn a land apart—while there's media coverage about Darfur, relatively little is actually being done on the ground.

Opportunities to serve others abound. We tend to gravitate toward causes that resonate with our own lives, while the needs of developing countries are perhaps more closely aligned with our innate sense of moral obligation. If this moral indicator is ignored, then the world must hold down its head in downright shame.

The Third World kitchen taught me that what matters most is not where you start in life or where you end up—the distance between the two is what really counts, measured by what we did for others while maintaining our own integrity and decency. I now go to my pantry of choices every day, where I continue to find the ingredients to make a difference. I have also learned how to blend those ingredients together.

Best of all, I've learned that appearances are, indeed, often deceiving. Despite their poverty, the vast majority of the people I've met in emerging nations persevere with a sense of pride and dignity.

The Third World has additionally taught me that you get out of a meal what you put into it, but what you leave out is just as important. Wholesome, fresh ingredients—when combined creatively and prepared with joy and passion—result in a satisfying meal. But too many rich ingredients, too many spices—or even a small amount of the wrong spice—can spoil a meal. Likewise, deciding which people, possessions, experiences, and endeavors are important to us—and which are not—goes a long way toward building a full and satisfying life.

The common ingredients of each day should be accepting personal accountability and responsibility for all of our actions, and the consequences should help us to learn more about ourselves in order to better ourselves. Whether we achieve the ultimate soufflé or we urge it to rise to no avail, our choices and our actions determine the outcome. And how the recipe turned out yesterday has little to do with its outcome today—unless, of course, there was something to be learned, which will make today's meal a little more palatable.

The developing world has also taught me that life, like food, tastes better when it's fresh. With everything in life, there are some things left over— whether in friendships, business relationships, romantic relationships, or even the relationship we have to ourselves. But what we served yesterday, or what transpired yesterday, is not the same today. If leftovers were so wonderful, we would make everything the day before, heat it up, and then serve it.

Put another way, we should endeavor to offer our very best at the most appropriate time. The leftovers in our lives are the events, actions, and emotions of yesterday—but what happened yesterday is gone. *Life's too short for leftovers.*

Bon Appétit

"Example is not the main thing in influencing others. It is the only thing."
~Albert Schweitzer

I have surrounded myself with Chef's nurturing wisdom every day since his ghostlike face appeared before my sheepish eyes on that memorable evening in 1992. I am forever grateful to Noel for keeping me close, transforming the course of my life. He welcomed me into his kitchen as a friend and "closet chef" to learn the finer touches of his culinary expertise … and to understand his deeper mission. I learned how to scramble eggs without using any utensil except the pan, and I endeavored to give of myself to help him offer the children of Africa a better tomorrow. He was my mentor and friend on a much deeper level than anyone else in my life. As a mentor, he schooled me for hours on end; and as a friend, he scolded and embraced me with equal vigor.

For many years, I was a student in Noel's kitchen of wisdom, where the apron of his profession had become the very fabric of his life. The kitchen that we both shared was not limited to this country, but boiled over into the Third World, where every child has a right to live, to have enough to eat, and to be respected as a human being.

I will never graduate, because there is no graduation ceremony; I will never receive a diploma, because there is no diploma. But what I achieved in Noel's kitchen is a degree of hope that I can make a meaningful difference in the lives of others—after changing my own life first. I took a sharp knife and burst the bubble that had become the gilded cage I'd lived in since my arrival from the shores of Jolly Olde England. Since then, I've made a point of surrounding myself with people wiser than me.

This book intends to illustrate how changing our lives enriches our lives. Think of the times when we sit for a long period of time and one leg starts to fall asleep; we adjust our bodies to feel more comfortable. In the big picture, life is no different. We usually only change when we are uncomfortable. But it doesn't have to be that way.

Some cooks only replace a menu item when it's run its course. But the great chefs are always changing their menus. Whether because they are tuned in to seasonal influences or because they know they have so much more to offer, they are not afraid to add or remove something. They believe in themselves enough to make those kinds of decisions.

Changing when we're comfortable means taking responsibility early enough to avoid discomfort. We can change even when things are going well. We can't change yesterday's menu; we can only change today's.

"Only a fool trips on what is behind him."
~Proverb

Of course, there are some things that stand the test of time, like Chef Noel's *Penne Bagutta with Chicken, Mushrooms and Broccoli,* or *Life with Integrity, Accountability, Love, and Decency.* Both are abidingly satisfying.

The nine lessons set forth herein pertain to the emotions and interactions that we all face in our daily lives. The lessons evolved as a result of me sitting down around the fire with people of the Third World, listening to their voices that collectively resound with wisdom and love. Like most of us, they want better lives for their families, and are prepared to do what it takes to get there. It's just a little more difficult when they are dealing with the particular challenges that life has put on their table.

These lessons slice across the cutting board of life—from the relationships we have to ourselves to the relationships we have with others.

By taking a hard look at your motives and the motives of others in *Read the Recipe* to observing the temperature at which you're functioning as you *Preheat the Oven*, you will begin to understand. In learning patience, forgiveness, and tolerance as you *Simmer, Don't Stir*, and in overcoming procrastination as you *Clean Your Plate*, you will begin to understand. In simplifying your life as you Just *Add Water*, you will continue to understand. You will begin to exceed your seeming limitations as you *Bring to a Boil*, and offer life's riches to others as you *Pass the Butter*. You will discover that you can make a difference in your world by getting to know your own kitchen ... and then inviting others in, who are part of the world we share.

These nine lessons are ones that matter. They will have a quiet way of sneaking into everyday life. We will never go hungry if we accept personal responsibility, and neither will the people around us. We may not see now that change is on the menu, but we will find ourselves ordering it.

We'll never know how far the ripples will travel or how many lives we might touch unless we drop the first potato into the water. Whether it's the taste of our own enriched lives or that of others, it's a dish that we'll order time and time again. We should spice our own lives the way we intend them to taste—we have all the right ingredients, and we are about to learn how to use them. With these lessons, we can choose a life the way we would choose a meal: wisely.

HORS D'OEUVRES

LESSON 1

Read the Recipe –
Open Your Eyes

"If you could kick the person in the pants for most of your trouble, you wouldn't sit for a month."
~Theodore Roosevelt

We're all brought into this world without being consulted, and most of us leave this world without choosing to—and what happens in between is all too often someone else's "fault"!

How quick we are to place blame on others without first seeing, and then understanding, ourselves. Three questions provide insight—and a measuring stick—on where we stand and where we fall; ask them in discussing any relationship between ourselves and others and we soon learn that the answers are the key ingredients to understanding:

1.   What do we bring to the table?
2.   What are our motives?
3.   What are we not saying?

We make demands of everyone else around us, but rarely of ourselves. If our house is on fire, we expect the fire department to be there immediately. If our house is being robbed, we demand that the police arrive quickly. If only we made the same demands of ourselves.

But day-to-day accountability to ourselves, like a recipe, only works if there is an understandable order to it. In an ideal world, we can bring order to our lives when we become self-aware; in the real world, however, that's usually a struggle. Sooner or later, most of us run into situations that are too big to handle. In the world in which we find ourselves, we can often avoid or navigate those situations; but people in the Third World don't have the same options. That divide leads both worlds to the most remarkable self-discoveries.

We must be able to read our own label of ingredients before we can read others', as therein lie the motives that govern our own outlook and subsequent actions. When we read other people, we are in fact looking first at what they bring to the table—their past, in particular. A person's history usually reveals the here and now. A potluck meal without everyone bringing something of substance is not a meal. If our motive is to have a genuine relationship with someone, then the best we can do is work on our own contribution to the feast.

Our actions very often lead to emotional stability or instability on our part. We can't control or change any other person without their consent and very few people give it. Only when we attempt to "rescue" someone or something do we usually take a controlling stance. In all kinds of relationships, we run the risk of becoming an "enabler," wherein lies little hope of a sustainable future.

In the Third World, so-called rescuing is looked upon from a different perspective. The motive to rescue can have an incredible and meaningful presence, as long as there is a conscious and intentional hand *up* and not a handout. Rescuing is usually found in "relief" efforts of countries assisting with immediate aid, but "development" is where the real truth and consequence are to be found.

Empowering the developing world with a taste of self-sufficiency is certainly a move in the right direction, but—to be successful—we must invite and include their voices along the way. They are the true and only measuring stick. What are the motives of the people who raise thousands of dollars to help with a specific cause? Are they interested in where the money actually goes, or do they simply feel they've done their part for the time being? Throughout the following lessons, we will observe that humanitarian aid is not the solution to most Third World problems. In fact, in many ways, aid is a deterrent to progress and does little to improve the big picture. As Karl Kraus said of Freudianism, "Aid is the disease of which it pretends to be the cure."

～

Other people's motives are often what determine our likes or dislikes toward them. Having knowledge of their motives is helpful in whether we decide to associate with them, respect them, or even like them. We certainly had all the facts in front of us when we decided that President Omar Hassan al-Bashir of Sudan was not someone we would like to have over for dinner. The International Criminal Court in The Hague, however, saw fit to invite him to appear at their dining table to see their special of the day: justice. The motives of one individual can differ from another, also depending upon circumstance. So, too, the motives of an individual in the Third World very often differ—usually by necessity— from those of us in the First World.

The motives of the Hutu tribe in Rwanda were completely void of compassion when they failed humanity by slaughtering their Tutsi neighbors, a group marked for extermination. The motive of the Janjaweed in Sudan (a government-sponsored militia that attacks innocents on the ground) was to continue the carnage—the United Nations estimated in 2013 an estimated 300,000 people were killed, and nearly two million were displaced. Other attacks came from government forces by air.

Survival is a motive that few of us can—or ever need to—comprehend. The motives of the Ethiopians were to find food, stay alive, and become productive members of their race; the motive of many of the refugees in Kenya's Kakuma refugee camp, close to the Sudanese border, was not to leave. Why should they return to Sudan where life was still barren and fingers were pointing at them for leaving? I witnessed first-hand in Kakuma how individuals who had fled the civil war in Sudan made new lives for themselves. The authorities in the camp, however, made those lives more difficult again, forcing refugees to leave. What began at 100,000 refugees went down to 60,000.

~

Destinations are everywhere. Whether it's a distant country such as Ethiopia, Rwanda, or Sudan that is in need of change, or whether it's a decision to change your own life, there is a need to realize that there is both relief and development. When we witness acts of nature that devastate cities, regions, and countries, we respond with a yearning to help—we donate time, or money, or both. Providing such immediate relief is sometimes referred to as a handout. Development, however—referred to as a hand up—is often left to far fewer individuals, the ones who go the distance.

"Glamour" aid only goes so far. Long-term investment is what the people of emerging nations need most of all. If only we can divert such investment away from government interference and corruption. In bypassing bureaucratic strongholds, we can help take away much of the corruption that still exists. People to People is empowerment and entrepreneurism; Government to Government is bureaucracy at its worst.

～

People are sometimes there for us when a relationship has ended or a business deal has fallen through, or when there's been a family tragedy. True friends are there for the long haul, not just a shoulder to cry on during those initial moments of acute anguish. We might look at the people who are in our lives as falling into two categories. One is the survival group, or—as

I like to call them—the *Pots and Pans*. The others are acquaintances, or the *Kitchen Pantry*. The *Pots and Pans* are those we would invite to be in our wedding; the *Kitchen Pantry* are the ones we would invite to be at our wedding. We will always be able to count on the *Pots and Pans* as being durable and loyal; the *Kitchen Pantry* will usually have to be restocked from time to time. Look at the times you have asked people to help you move. The *Kitchen Pantry* will say "yes," but it's the *Pots and Pans* who actually show up.

As long as we understand and realize people's motives, we have the knowledge to make choices. Never try and store the *Pots and Pans* in the *Kitchen Pantry*. In Ethiopia, for example, I met a family that had only the most basic food of injera pancakes— yet they made the most of it without the help of other ingredients. Their needs were met and their survival was complete ... at least until the next meal. Similarly, it has often been said that people come into our lives for a season, a reason, or a lifetime; the *Pots and Pans* are there for a lifetime, and we should never take them for granted.

~

The aprons we wear in the kitchen are like the different masks we wear every day—we often hide behind them. I have attempted at times to call myself a chef, only to realize that dressing the part does not necessarily make me the part. I have even struggled to earn the distinction of cook, no matter the apron I wear.

The masks we wear don't necessarily make us real—and being real is what we should strive for. In the beloved children's book, *The Velveteen Rabbit*, by Margery Williams, the Rabbit asks the Straw Horse, "What makes you real?" to which the horse replies, "When someone loves you." To be real is to love ourselves first, and then to be loved by others. Usually, it's here that the *Kitchen Pantry* becomes apparent.

We should not attempt to prove others wrong but, instead, prove ourselves right. Doing so allows people to see what we are truly made of—what makes us real—and what our true motives are.

Before we put on a mask or an apron, we must first look in the mirror and ask ourselves what role we are going to play in our own lives today. We wear many different masks at different times of the day. We play the role of mother, father, friend, employer, employee, counselor, lover, and so on. We will also be in the kitchen serving up different meals at different times. But sometimes we forget to really taste what we have cooked; indeed, sometimes it's better that we can't remember how it tasted. Too often, we spend too much time analyzing life instead of living it. Wrong ingredients, undercooked, overcooked ... you know the feeling.

The problem with wearing so many masks is that—at the end of the day—you don't know who you really are. When you take off the final mask, you will see the real you—whom you sleep with and wake up to. Before going to bed, then, we should make it a habit to look in the mirror again and ask ourselves one simple, but revealing, question: "How many times have I lied to myself today?" Not to others, but to ourselves.

Likewise, before we read a book or magazine in bed, we should reread ourselves. We promised we were going to the gym after coffee, but we never arrived at the gym. We promised we would volunteer, but we just didn't get around to it. We promised we would work to change ourselves for the better, but we just forgot. We need to be true to ourselves. We are only as loud as our voice, and as strong as our actions.

If we can get through a day without lying to ourselves, there's a wonderful chance that this honesty will carry over to others with whom we come into contact. How do some politicians look at themselves in the mirror and truly like what they see, when the true reflection is one of deception? Sudan cried out for help and we offered only broken promises, wrapped up in years of trying to figure out all the ingredients necessary when they needed only one … peace. When we take politics out of the equation, all we are left with is common sense.

One of the most insightful and powerful writings I've ever come across is Charles Finn's poem, "Please Hear What I'm Not Saying." I have included it here because it would be a major omission, and one I would regret not sharing:

> *Don't be fooled by me.*
> *Don't be fooled by the face I wear*
> *for I wear a mask, a thousand masks,*
> *masks that I'm afraid to take off,*
> *and none of them is me.*
>
> *Pretending is an art that's second nature with me,*
> *but don't be fooled,*
> *for God's sake don't be fooled.*
> *I give you the impression that I'm secure,*
> *that all is sunny and unruffled with me, within as*
> *well as without,*
> *that confidence is my name and coolness my game,*
> *that the water's calm and I'm in command*

and that I need no one,
but don't believe me.
My surface may seem smooth but my surface is
my mask,
ever-varying and ever-concealing.
Beneath lies no complacence.
Beneath lies confusion, and fear, and aloneness.
But I hide this. I don't want anybody to know it.
I panic at the thought of my weakness exposed.
That's why I frantically create a mask to hide
behind,
a nonchalant sophisticated facade,
to help me pretend,
to shield me from the glance that knows.

But such a glance is precisely my salvation, my
only hope,
and I know it.
That is, if it's followed by acceptance,
if it's followed by love.
It's the only thing that can liberate me from myself,
from my own self-built prison walls,
from the barriers I so painstakingly erect.
It's the only thing that will assure me
of what I can't assure myself,
that I'm really worth something.

But I don't tell you this. I don't dare to, I'm afraid to.
I'm afraid your glance will not be followed by
acceptance,
will not be followed by love.
I'm afraid you'll think less of me,
that you'll laugh, and your laugh would kill me.
I'm afraid that deep-down I'm nothing
and that you will see this and reject me.

So I play my game, my desperate pretending game,
with a facade of assurance without
and a trembling child within.
So begins the glittering but empty parade of masks,
and my life becomes a front.
I idly chatter to you in the suave tones of surface
talk.
I tell you everything that's really nothing,
and nothing of what's everything,
of what's crying within me.
So when I'm going through my routine
do not be fooled by what I'm saying.
Please listen carefully and try to hear what I'm
not saying,
what I'd like to be able to say,
what for survival I need to say,
but what I can't say.

I don't like hiding.
I don't like playing superficial phony games.
I want to stop playing them.
I want to be genuine and spontaneous and me
but you've got to help me.
You've got to hold out your hand
even when that's the last thing I seem to want.
Only you can wipe away from my eyes
the blank stare of the breathing dead.
Only you can call me into aliveness.
Each time you're kind, and gentle, and encouraging,
each time you try to understand because you really
care,
my heart begins to grow wings—
very small wings,
very feeble wings,
but wings!

With your power to touch me into feeling
you can breathe life into me.
I want you to know that.
I want you to know how important you are to me,
how you can be a creator—an honest-to-God
creator—
of the person that is me
if you choose to.

You alone can break down the wall behind which
I tremble,
you alone can remove my mask,
you alone can release me from my shadow-world
of panic,
from my lonely prison,
if you choose to.
Please choose to.

Do not pass me by.
It will not be easy for you.
A long conviction of worthlessness builds strong
walls.
The nearer you approach to me the blinder I may
strike back.
It's irrational, but despite what the books say
about man
often I am irrational.
I fight against the very thing I cry out for.
But I am told that love is stronger than strong walls
and in this lies my hope.
Please try to beat down those walls
with firm hands but with gentle hands
for a child is very sensitive.

Who am I, you may wonder?
I am someone you know very well.

For I am every man you meet
and I am every woman you meet.

Accountability leads to self-respect and—ultimately—the respect of others. It's a wonderful feeling when others both like and respect us, as most of us have a desire for acceptance; and, yes, we do take things personally. How many times have we heard, "It's not what you know, but whom you know"? I take it a few steps further by adding, "It's who knows you and likes you."

Looking a person in the eye and telling them we won't do something instead of we can't do something is more honest ... and more respected. If we can't do something, they will usually find someone who can. How many lives would have been saved in the Rwandan genocide if the United Nations would have had the intestinal fortitude to say we *won't* do anything to save lives, instead of we *can't*? It would have been then that the world could have found someone who could. The respect is in the conviction of why we believe we can or won't ... not in the can't. Very few cooks will tell us they can't make toast. They very often can, or they won't.

Most people in emerging nations have little conception of different masks, or how they're perceived by the rest of the world. Very few have even a mirror to look into; instead, they look inside of themselves, where a reflection of despair and anguish is their special of the day. Their very existence is one of survival and nurturing. How they respond to their circumstances provides a lesson for all of us—they are dignified in an undignified world. They have each other, and that in itself is the foundation on which they build a life each and every day.

Their family of pots and pans offers true hope, love, and a realness that much of the rest of the world could only hope to experience. Admittedly, they are lacking in so many things that the majority of this world takes for granted. We have the most satisfying table set before us on which we can feast. If only we would, for one minute, sit down with them at that same table and listen to what they are *not* saying.

Their silence can teach us so much. When we but look into their eyes, we can begin to understand them—the goodness of their souls and the depths of their spirits. How ironic that some of the poorest people on earth can sometimes be the happiest.

The thought of food in the stomach of any child in Ethiopia brings a smile to my face, and a child who is fed has a similar, but more satisfied, smile. The thought of reconciliation and peace in the hearts of many a child in Rwanda also brings hope to my heart, as a child who is at peace is usually at peace with others.

The children who survived the Rwandan genocide learned what other parents did to their parents. But instead of seeing the children pick up those same knives and machetes to retaliate through a similar carnage, we witnessed how sports and the arts can bring about playful harmony that, in turn, helps forge a lasting peace.

In Rwanda, I saw just how far these children have come when the local headmaster at the school where I was leading a soccer clinic pointed out that the field we were on—this very field where children were now playing and laughing—was the same field were more than 200 children were macheted to death. That moment never left me, and has become yet another watershed that pushes me to continue doing what I can with what I have to help. We can't be all things to all people, but we can be one thing to one child. We can be there for them.

The motives of the Rwandan children are different now, as time has somewhat healed their physical and psychological wounds. They now look to build themselves up from within, even as their country is building itself back up from without.

In Sudan, just living through a day is the primary objective. People there can't think about education, self-sufficiency, or even a future when—for the immediate moment—their chief concern is preserving their lives, and the lives of their loved ones. Every day, they awake to the threat of murder and rape, and—even if they elude bullets or machetes—the onset of disease and starvation is ever-present.

In his essay "The Paradox of Our Time," Bob Moorehead captures how our motives can sometimes get distorted, and how the consequences thereof hopefully lead us to read the recipe in order to prepare for transformation:

> *"The paradox of our time in history is that we have taller buildings but shorter tempers, wider freeways, but narrower viewpoints. We spend more, but have less, we buy more, but enjoy less. We have bigger houses and smaller families, more conveniences, but less time. We have more degrees but less sense, more knowledge, but less judgment, more experts, yet more problems, more medicine, but less wellness.*
>
> *We drink too much, smoke too much, spend too recklessly, laugh too little, drive too fast, get too angry, stay up too late, get up too tired, read*

too little, watch TV too much, and pray too seldom. We have multiplied our possessions, but reduced our values. We talk too much, love too seldom, and hate too often.

We've learned how to make a living, but not a life. We've added years to life not life to years. We've been all the way to the moon and back, but have trouble crossing the street to meet a new neighbor. We conquered outer space but not inner space. We've done larger things, but not better things.

We've cleaned up the air, but polluted the soul. We've conquered the atom, but not our prejudice. We write more, but learn less. We plan more, but accomplish less. We've learned to rush, but not to wait. We build more computers to hold more information, to produce more copies than ever, but we communicate less and less.

These are the times of fast foods and slow digestion, big men and small character, steep profits and shallow relationships.

These are the days of two incomes but more divorce, fancier houses, but broken homes ..."

We should remember to read the recipe to identify what is needed to make it more complete. We should read ourselves to see what is needed to make ourselves more complete. And then we can go on to read others to perhaps help them make their lives more complete. We might have advanced beyond where we started in life, but most of us have not gone as far as we can go. To begin, we merely have to open our eyes and take in the view.

LESSON 2

Preheat the Oven –
Check Your Temperature

"A leader is a dealer in hope."
~Napoleon Bonaparte

N ow that we have the ingredients from the recipe, we can begin to prepare our meal—but we need our oven to be at the right temperature to be successful. Different stoves in different parts of the world will have varied results. We might overcook the meal, undercook it, or—even worse—never get it started.

So, too, different people in different regions of the world have differing outcomes in their daily lives. At just the right temperature we can become leaders, as long as we understand that principles of leadership must ensure equality, and that you can't lead if conversion is your goal. Authentic leadership is a relationship, not a goal unto itself.

Leadership isn't about talent—but about freeing talent in others. Put another way, leadership is often looked at as being a directional tool to help others. We can't all be good leaders, however, as we've learned from man's inhumanity to man through war. In Sudan's and Rwanda's pasts, leadership brought on human misery and destruction. The plan we have for ourselves is not always the same plan we have for others ... or that others have for us.

> *"I am more afraid of an army of 100 sheep led by a lion than an army of 100 lions led by a sheep."*
> ~Charles Maurice de Talleyrand

Leadership thrives with healthy motives. As Lloyd Lewan—a dear and close friend, and one of the most descent men and leaders I know—once said:

> *"Show me a church filled with kids; I'll show you a theologian and leader in the pulpit. Show me a restaurant with a crowd; I'll show you a chef and leader in the kitchen.*
> *Show me a class always over-enrolled; I'll show you a teacher and leader in the classroom. Show me a good family, I'll show you parents and leaders in the home."*

Never did I observe this principle more intensely than in the schools of Ethiopia and Rwanda. Historically, Rwandans—mostly undereducated, ignorant and poor—are known to follow authority. So when they were ordered to kill, they obeyed.

"Victory has a thousand fathers, but defeat is an orphan."
~John F. Kennedy

In Ethiopia, there was no authority unless you invited an act of nature to the table. Famine ran rampant for years. Women and girls would walk hours for water to bring home, and for eucalyptus firewood to be sold in city markets for a few dollars. Returning home with the water and a pittance, they survived ... day by day, week by week, until months turned into years. But this doesn't have to be their life or their legacy ... things are changing now as new leaders are beginning to emerge.

Education is becoming more prevalent as many developing countries are checking their own temperatures and recognizing that there can't be forward progress without education as the foundation on which to build a future. Even now, with this knowledge, more attention must be given to girls—not only boys.

In Rwanda after the start of the new millennium, more than 49% of the lower Parliament were women, and that's good news—because educating women will help decrease HIV/AIDS, and education brings empowerment to make choices for one's own life. It's well-known that many HIV-positive men in tribal cultures believe that if they have intercourse with a virgin they will themselves become pure. We can't delay in filling classrooms with girls!

That said, one challenge in some Third World educational settings is that kindergarten doesn't exist. When children reach the primary school level at seven years of age, the basics have been omitted from their development. But with an educated mother, who has herself been through a school system, hope prevails that her children might receive some rudimentary education *before* age seven.

Speaking of checking our temperatures ... enough of aid to developing countries. It doesn't work and never will. We are preheating the oven with utter disregard as to what temperature should be set. In the past fifty years, according to Dambisa Moyo in her book, *Dead Aid*, more than $1 trillion in development-related aid has been given by rich countries to Africa. They are no better off today because these countries have never even seen a thermometer to gauge the current temperature, let alone known how to use one.

"Go to the people. Live with them. Learn from them. Love them. Start with what they know. Build with what they have. But with the best leaders, when the work is done, the task accomplished, the people will say 'We have done this ourselves.'"
~Lao Tzu

Response to the cries of emerging nations is all too often determined by what others feel they need, which isn't necessarily what they *actually* need. Even when aid is freely given to a country, it indirectly supports the corrupt governments that are often responsible for a country's miserable conditions ... instead of directly helping its people. As a result, trust between the people and those who provide aid is compromised.

~

Preheating your own personal oven allows you to prepare for making the world—and your own life—a little better by understanding that your contribution, however humble, can still be significant. We can't all help empower the Third World the way governments and institutions attempt to; but we can do a better job of realizing our role in the lives of others. People in developing countries don't want us continually interfering with areas of their lives that we don't understand—just as we wouldn't want to interfere in other peoples' business here in our own neighborhoods.

So we help where we can, then step back and reevaluate. Helping out can come in numerous ways, geared to the calling of different situations. In the Third World, the scope of aid occurs on three levels:

1. **Humanitarian aid:** immediately dispersed in response to catastrophes;

2. **Charity-based aid:** on-the-ground services and disbursements from charities; and

3. **Systematic aid**: government assistance from other governments or institution.

In our own lives, assistance comes in three forms of support, temporarily or for the long-term:

1. **Listening:** allowing others to share their feelings and emotions;

2. **Talking:** sharing our personal insights and input; and

3. **Acting:** putting hands and feet toward doing something for someone else.

Of course, we can only work with—and for—others when we have an understanding of ourselves. This understanding often occurs when we, too, have experienced a similar situation ... or we've seen it repeat itself time and again with others.

An oven at just the right temperature can produce a leader with just the right values. While those values are largely the same for men and women in our world, differences abound in the Third World. For starters, leadership should not be sexist. Gender does not unleash ability, leadership does. Leadership identifies, frees, encourages, and guides human talent. It does not control, restrict, or diminish talent.

Equality is a term that, in many foreign cultures, has never really surfaced—but it is a reality that we must awaken and encourage. In the Third World, especially, the roles of men and woman are clearly defined, and little has changed over the years; but now, by helping girls attend school as early as possible, we pave the way for them to become future leaders in their communities, their countries, and the world.

There are two things that make someone successful. The first is that you never reveal everything you know. The second is ... well ... I don't want to say. Daniel Deng Bol Aruai was such an individual. He would give you only so much about himself and his upbringing. He did, however, exude passion about his cause for the world.

He first contacted me about doing some soccer coaching in Kenya. *Kenya*, I pondered. *Another African country with a calling?*

I ignored his first and second requests. Checking my own temperature, I simply didn't feel like the time was right ... and I didn't want to take away from what I was already doing. I had enough on my plate with my work in Ethiopia and Rwanda. Wearing too many hats—or masks or aprons, as the case may be— can have the negative effect of watering down one's original intents.

But Daniel continued to pester me until, finally, I bowed to his passion and perseverance. Daniel was one of the first Lost Boys of Sudan to leave Sudan and be allowed to live in the United States. The exodus of 5,000 individuals (only 80 of which were girls) was a fresh start into unfamiliar territory.

I had always been fascinated by this country— relentless in its quest for peace, but never quite achieving that goal. They had tried, but "try" is a reflection of a past failure. Either you do or you don't. And in the past they hadn't.

The Sudanese government was an Arab dictator- ship. Ethnic Africans had suffered discrimination for years. They rebelled in 2003 when the government moved to exterminate them. A boiling pot filled to the brim with genocide intent was now taken off the back burner. Muslims in the north and Christians in the south. Oil in the south, little in the north. And let's not forget the Black Muslims in the western region we know as Darfur. They have been ruthlessly persecuted by Muslim leaders who wanted a pure Muslim race.

We never heard much about Sudan. Instead, Darfur became the celebrity cause for reaching out to help abolish such hatred. In this case, people who might be labeled part of the "Glamour Aid" group—Mia Farrow, Don Cheadle, George Clooney, Sir Richard Branson, John Prendergast, and others—never put down the torch or relinquished the gauntlet to help bring about peace. They are a lighthouse to the poor and persecuted there.

I was fortunate to be asked to speak in San Francisco in 2008 on the only leg of the Olympic Torch that went through the United States on its way to Beijing. I was a member of Team Darfur, a group of amateur and professional athletes from around the world who believed in the cause for common good and peace in Darfur. As I stood on the steps of the Ferry Building on the Embarcadero Public Promenade before thousands of Chinese, Tibetans, and Sudanese peacemakers, my moment had arrived. I was now a dealer in hope.

I seized the opportunity to echo the years of suffering through the bullhorn in my hand, my instrument of truth. I could now make a difference with words, although I never thought they'd make national news. But they did ... and for that one fleeting moment, I felt as a true leader would. Not because of who I was, because I was only a voice, but because I believed as Bonaparte had said—that my words could help point the way toward a hopeful future:

> *"Today before us all, we will witness a gathering of cultures and beliefs. In the Olympics, we are judged on time, distance, height, and subjectivity by individuals we have never met. Yet beyond the accolades of bronze, silver, or gold will remain our voices, which will outlive any piece of metal— no matter how it is coated or presented. Let us turn the pedestal of our accomplishments into a platform of change and a beacon of light that others can always count on ... no matter how dark the days seem."*

There, I had shared my belief. I turned and handed the bullhorn to a new friend and Hollywood figure, Maria Bello. She smiled and whispered, "You've done this before, haven't you?" If only I had, then perhaps that hope could have come a little earlier. The train was leaving the station ... I jumped on the caboose and, every day since then, I've been working my way up to the engine to help lead others.

Ever since my British homeland gave independence to Sudan in 1956, the military regimes have favored Islamic-oriented governments, which have dominated its national politics. Sudan was embroiled in two long civil wars—the first ended in 1972, but broke out again in 1983; this second was devastating, with four million displaced and two million dead over two decades of war and famine.

Peace talks began to move forward between 2002 and 2004; the last peace treaty was signed in January 2005, bringing the Southern Christians autonomy for six years. In 2011, the South voted for an independent country by a landslide. But in 2003, Darfur broke out in war and refugees fled into Chad. It was a fight over land and water by low-level tribes that erupted into large-scale violence when they blamed the Muslim government in Khartoum for neglecting them. Not only did they ignore what was going on in this area of Western Sudan, but this same government incited and ignited further bloodshed by forming the Janjaweed (Arab tribal militia) to persecute, rape, and kill.

These young boys were given horses, camels, and guns, which falsely empowered them toward destructive ends. If only they would have applied the gift of empowerment from a positive source and for a constructive purpose, we might be talking less about war and more about peace. These boys had little notion of right or wrong. If you know no different, you know no better ... and you can't make a difference until you put aside differences. They were indoctrinated and led without a conscience.

~

On May 15, 1983, in the village of Bor, Daniel and his family were huddled around the fire listening to a wise elder predict that war would be coming the following day. Daniel's mother heeded the warning as truth and quickly proceeded to pack food and supplies, which she rushed to hide in a forested area. At 5 a.m. the following day, the first bullet of this second civil war pierced the crisp morning air. It was time.

Daniel's mother gathered up the family and swiftly moved toward that same clump of trees where, the night before, she had begun to prepare for their future. As they got close to the forest, a mortar shell skimmed over their heads and landed precisely where the provisions were hidden, destroying everything but their spirits. They shifted plans and began an exodus to Ethiopia and Kenya—they improvised a path that the rest of the world would follow, only by reading about it. Famine and crocodile-infested waters prevented many from reaching any kind of safe destination. So began the plight of the Lost Boys of the Sudan.

Daniel was separated from his mother. Despite not knowing her fate, he pressed on to become one of the first refugees to enter Kenya's Kakuma camp in Turkana County. Kakuma is Swahili for "nowhere," which epitomizes the seclusion of the region. Daniel led many by example, although he first thought the camp might be a dangerous trap; that was before he learned that Kenya is one of the most generous countries in the world when it comes to hosting refugees, the majority of which have come from Sudan.

Back in the States, Daniel tried to explain all of this, but I wanted none of it. I was busy. He persisted, however, and when he began to explain that more than 100,000 refugees where originally accommodated there, I began to take note—my temperature was beginning to be tested by an unknown, pestering individual whom I now realize is as much a leader as anyone I have ever known. He wanted to go home, and he wanted me to go with him.

MAIN COURSE

LESSON 3

Rare, Medium or Well – Realize Your Choices

*"In the end that was the choice you made,
and it doesn't matter how hard it was to make it.
It matters that you did."*
~Cassandra Clare, *City of Glass*

Too often in life, some of us pass blame to others and look for excuses to avoid responsibility. But, in the words of Christopher Pike, "When you point your finger at someone, anyone, it is often a moment of judgment. We point our fingers when we want to scold someone, point out what they have done wrong. But each time we point, we simultaneously point three fingers back at ourselves."

Daniel had made a choice to reach out to me with the purest of intentions—despite my initial reservations, his motives turned out to be good, and his reasoning sound. I just had to meet him to see what he was all about and what drove him. Little did I know then that he drove himself, in more ways than one.

He was coming up to Denver from Dallas, where he now lived, and he was arriving on a Saturday. I missed his first phone call; on calling back the number, I reached the downtown Greyhound bus terminal. *Strange*, I thought. I assumed he was flying (I found out later that he didn't have the money to fly). The next call from Daniel brought about our real first connection. He proved he was good for his word, and that follow-through was important to him.

I arranged to meet Daniel at an Ethiopian restaurant on Colfax Avenue that afternoon. "How will I recognize you?" was the first question I asked. In a five-minute call—in which little was said, but much was revealed—he replied, "I'll be the one in the wheelchair." *Wheelchair?* I was dumbfounded. How could someone who had been running for years be in a wheelchair, and how could he lead me in Sudan? He reassured me as best he could that it's not where you're "standing" in life that's important, but the view you have from it. I was speechless, humbled, and intrigued—all within the first few spoken words between us.

I pulled up to the restaurant and there he was, "standing tall" in his wheelchair, with a smile that everybody could love, not just his mother. Speaking of mothers, they were the subject of our first verbal spars. Daniel hadn't seen his mother since he fled his village, but now it was time. Underneath his tough exterior, he was soft inside—especially when it came to his mother. You build up resilience over time ... and the calluses on Daniel's hands showed some of what he'd gone through, pushing his way through life.

He hinted that it would be good for my soul to go with him. "Sure," I insisted sarcastically. Nothing more refreshing than going on a 25,000-kilometer roundtrip journey aboard twelve flights just to say, "Here's your mom. Now can I go home?" We're not talking about Rwanda, where at least you can visit the gorillas in Volcano National Park, or dine at my favorite restaurant—Republika's—in Kigali. Instead, Daniel and I were talking about traveling to one of the most dangerous places in Africa, right up there with the Republic of the Congo.

"We can first stop in Kakuma, and you can see what all the sadness is about." Sadness and danger weren't part of any itinerary I imagined for myself, yet Daniel reassured me over and again that we'd be safe. How can you feel safe when you are embarking on a journey to a destination that so many wanted to get away from ... as fast as they could? It was similar to when you win a long drive contest at golf, and they give you a new driver for the prize. You really don't need a new driver if you just hit the longest golf ball with the old one. I was quite happy staying at home.

Daniel was trying to persuade me that, if he felt safe returning, then so could I. But I insisted that I would stay one step behind and follow in his tracks, so to speak. He had been a leader of boys at one stage of his life, and now he was to embark as a leader of men—albeit that one of them was a rather nervous and hesitant man, certainly at this stage of the game.

～

I had been nervous about travel at one other time in my life. It was when I decided to leave America and head back to England to continue an honors course at the University of Bradford. While I'd graduated in three years, I had the opportunity to return for an additional degree. This had been my second trip to the United States and, after six weeks at Penn State University, I had to choose. Should I stay in this wonderful country or return home to yet another wonderful country? Walter Bahr, with whom I wrote my first book on soccer, gave me my first real opportunity in the United States. After my six weeks of discovery learning, he offered me a coaching position and the chance to earn a master's at the university.

I was overwhelmed by what I'd experienced in Pennsylvania—the people, especially, made me feel welcome. I was a guest of the United States, which I never took for granted—when you're in someone else's home, you respect that privilege.

It was a Monday evening, the night before I was supposed to leave early for Philadelphia to take my flight home to London's Heathrow airport. I was still unsure whether to go or stay put, but I knew I had to make a decision—right or wrong. My family and known lifestyle back in England, or a life here in the states that few Brits would risk everything for. The British are set in their ways, and they don't really like change. You might call it stubborn. We have been called a lot worse throughout history.

Walter took me into his office and looked me straight in the eyes. "I have the answer," he said softly. For the first time in days, I felt as if a cloak of calm was being slowly draped around me—but it was short-lived. "We'll toss a coin." I started to sweat. "What the heck do you mean, 'toss a coin?'" My whole future was riding on the spin cycle of a quarter! But I was running out of time. My bags were packed and my Greyhound bus ticket had already been purchased.

Heads I stayed, tails I would leave. As the quarter spun in the air, I knew this was a defining moment. Tails it was. "How about best out of three?" I said. "Go home, Michael," he said. I cried as I hugged one of my first true mentors in life. He gently tried to release me, but I wouldn't let him. I couldn't. My jacket button had locked with his lapel pin. "See?" I said loudly. "I'm not meant to leave." But it was useless. The verdict was in.

The ride to Philadelphia was about five hours. Much as I tried to look around at the passing beauty of the fall colors—perhaps for the last time—my watery eyes wouldn't allow it. I sat in a Burger King in central Philadelphia for six hours, contemplating whether I had made the right choice. Stay. Go. Stay. Or go. These were the specials of the day. Little did I know that fate would soon, bizarrely, make the choice for me.

I grabbed a taxi to the international terminal. Closing the door after getting out of the cab, I looked up at the large Pan Am sign. Almost home. Inside, a Pan Am attendant came out of nowhere and asked if I was on Flight 323 to Heathrow. "Yes, I am," I answered. "Is there a problem?" She motioned for me to quickly head over to the British Airways gate; my Pan Am flight had been cancelled due to an air traffic controllers' dispute in London. I was now on British Airways. "What about my two Adidas bags? I need to check them." The British Airways airline representative hurriedly explained that I didn't have time. The flight was leaving in thirty minutes.

I ran like they do in the movies when they portray a passenger who's late for a flight. I was the last person on, just before the door closed. No more time to think. I was going home ... or so I thought. After handing my bags to a flight attendant, she told me she would let me know when and where she found a space for them to be stowed. I went quickly to my seat, trying to ignore the glares from all the passengers already seated toward that one passenger who seems to hold up everyone's lives. Was fate trying to stall me and point me toward a different future, or was it simply that I couldn't find my seatbelt for the life of me? Finally, I found it beneath a sleeping child who was now wide awake.

The family was from Wayne, New Jersey. I learned that quickly as I attempted small talk with the couple to make up for me having woken their little boy out of a sleep that might have lasted the whole six hours to London. I ordered my evening meal, believing the next couple I would meet would be my parents on my arrival.

After settling in with my seatbelt firmly fastened, the pilot informed us that we would be landing in Boston to pick up a few more passengers. I broke out in a cold sweat. Was this a sign? What was I going to do, jump the plane? Would the same person running in the airport in Philadelphia also run on the tarmac next to the plane in Boston? I tried to nap, exhausted from all the events of the last forty-eight hours ... but adrenalin got the better of me.

We landed in Boston after a relatively short flight, and the few remaining passengers boarded. After everyone was seated, the flight attendant said over the intercom words that I have never forgotten: "Mr. Ditchfield, would you please come to the front of the plane? I will show you where your bags are stored." I got up, remembering this time to put my seatbelt where I could easily find it. I walked sheepishly down the aisle as if in slow motion, my fellow passengers looking to see who was delaying the flight this time. Yes, it was me again. Don't take a bow, I thought. Just get the information, and then hustle back to your adopted flight family from New Jersey. You have a long flight ahead of you with these people.

The flight attendant pointed out where my two bags were stowed. There they were, underneath the back of the last first-class seat, right next to the still-open door of the plane. I looked down at the bags, I looked at the open door, and then I turned to the flight attendant and smiled. I had just made the biggest and most decisive choice of my life. I handed her my ticket, picked up my bags, thanked her, and walked off the plane. She called after me that once I had disembarked, I couldn't return. That, apparently, was the plan all along—I just didn't know it at the time.

I never once looked back. "I guess this is your lucky day," I said to the little old lady waiting on standby for that flight. "No, this is *your* lucky day," she said, seeing the beaming smile on my face. Well, I guess it was.

I didn't think that day could get any more surreal, but it did. As I went over the recent events in my head, I realized it had all been meant to be. If my bags had been checked in Philadelphia, I couldn't have jumped that plane.

Watching the same plane that I was just on takeoff into the dusk again felt like being in a movie in which I was the leading man. But as I contemplated my next steps, I doubted myself. Not my choice to jump the plane, but my choice to order chicken instead of the steak ... at least I still had my sense of humor.

What the heck do I do now? No place to stay, no way back to Philadelphia, and no money. (I had converted my dollars into English currency already—all of it, that is, except for one quarter that I now believed meant something special.) I had made a choice all right.

As I started to pull myself together, I felt a tap on my shoulder. I turned around, thinking I was about to join a spiritual cult or buy a year's subscription to magazines that would keep on coming, no matter what I did to cancel them. Instead, and I kid you not, an older gentleman with a white beard looked me in the eye and asked if I was alright.

Was it that easy to observe my stunned state, or was it my not budging from the spot on the floor, as if claiming squatter's rights? After I explained all that had happened, the man chuckled. "Follow me," he said. I felt like a displaced disciple following him to the site of his next miracle. His name was Stephen W. Braham, and he was an international stamp dealer with the same accent as mine ... although his was perhaps a little more posh than my own. But I didn't need a translator, and I accepted him with open arms.

He was himself going to Philadelphia for a stamp exhibit, and he purchased a ticket for me on the same flight. The choice to stay was starting to take on a whole different meaning now, and when he got me my own room at the Sheraton in downtown Philly, I was convinced I was on the right track. *Bring on another miracle!* I was getting a little cocky now.

I asked Stephen why he had been so kind to a complete stranger. "Because, Michael, if my son was in the same situation as you, I would hope someone would do the same for him." My cockiness dissolved in an instant. There are decent people in this world, and I had just stumbled into one of them. I said good-night as I headed to my room, and that was the last time I ever saw Stephen. I did send him a thank-you letter a few days later ... it was the least I could do.

I called my parents in England that night. By this time, they were about to leave for the airport. I explained what had just taken place, and I broke the news that I had decided to stay in the United States. My mother began to cry, but after repeatedly asking the reason for her tears, she finally answered through sniffles, "Your breakfast is in the oven and it will be spoiled." I was 5,600 kilometers away and staying in a different country for good, and all my mum was concerned about was the bacon and eggs in the oven! English mum, indeed.

The next day, I took the same Greyhound route I had taken to get here, only this time I had no choices to make ... other than what I wanted for supper once I was home again in State College. The only other time I have discussed a ride on a Greyhound bus was with Daniel, many years later.

~

At first I pitied Daniel, based on what I saw and knew, but I soon realized it was what *he* knew and what *he* saw that was important. Heck, he probably looked me up and down and pitied me. I was dressed in a suit, with matching tie and socks. Even though we both wanted to hug, standing firm—and sitting firm—got the better of us. We simply shook each other's hands and smiled.

~

I had been hesitant twice before, although the circumstances had been a little different. Ethiopia was a choice Noel made for me. I had no input whatsoever. I was going, and that was that. Rwanda became a choice when I saw the horrific pictures that came out of a land that we—the West—let down terribly. Noel was asked to work in Rwanda, but he had a singleness of purpose and stayed true to his calling in Ethiopia ... and he wanted me to go out on my own. "Cut the apron strings and fly," he said. "I will continue to work in Ethiopia, but it's a big world out there. Now, go!" I was much happier keeping the apron strings tied tightly together and watching someone else deliver food—and hope. But he did it again, pushing me beyond my comfort zone. I never knew how, but I now know why.

I had never been to Africa before. For me, Africa was a destination for safaris—and, to be honest, the local zoo was sufficient for me to see the animals at a fraction of the cost of an airline ticket to Never Never

Land ("Never," because I never had any desire to go there at any time in my life). Africa just wasn't on my radar. What was Noel thinking when he chose Ethiopia?

Never wavering in his relentless mission to help children, Noel was thinking with his heart. It was his heart that delivered the beat for helping others, and sometimes his brain got in on the action, too. Indeed, some of his ideas were smart enough to bring about results.

"How about getting shoes for the children who have to walk two hours to school?" I proudly asked. "Their feet grow and they will be out of those shoes quicker than you can get them to wear them," Noel quickly retorted. "Plus, the soles of their feet will soften while they wear them. Any more brilliant ideas, Ditchfield?" I never mentioned footwear again.

~

Daniel seemed a lot nicer than Noel when we first met. His choices were along the lines of Noel's, but his was a different calling and Sudan was more dangerous. I knew I would never experience anything like this journey again, certainly not with Daniel in the driver's seat. So I became willing to join the experience of a boy who blew his own trumpet for salvation in his homeland; all I was offering was a place for myself in the rear of the orchestra, hoping this fanfare would perhaps culminate in an encore.

You never step into the same river twice, and this was never more evident than in Sudan. Ethiopia and Rwanda were in less of a survival mode at this stage of my humanitarian journey than Sudan—a country that had swapped a civil war between north and south for daily tragedies in Darfur. Here we were, to see if hope could make a difference. Once a decision is made, right or wrong, goals become clearer—and more attainable. As the Chinese proverb states, "The best time to plant a tree was twenty years ago. The next best time is now."

Daniel and Noel both chose to be lighthouses, not weathervanes. They chose to stand for something on firm ground. You could always count on them. Weathervanes change direction with every gust, as do many of us—thoughtlessly following the crowd; but Daniel and Noel, like lighthouses, never faltered. You could trust them and their stalwart commitment to decency and humanity. They were sturdy, and they held themselves accountable to this earth and the people of all colors and cultures who are nourished by it.

～

Daniel was about ready for his show-and-tell. His callused hands were now pushing him toward his mother's smile and warm embrace. He was about to show his family and friends in the village all that can be accomplished from his perspective, and how they can move in the same direction—albeit with seemingly better traction. He was setting a standard that others would be wise to uphold, and tracks that would be easy to follow.

Daniel's family did not choose to be poor, nor did they choose war. What they did choose was the will to survive. If not for the random fortune of the human lottery, any one of us might have been born on the other side of the world. A world we know little about, and have seemingly little in common with ... or they with us. But we can choose to help, or we should, if our moral compass is directed toward our true north.

Of all the choices that confront the poor of the Third World, the one I admire most—and am most humbled by—is the choice they make to be happy. Admittedly, they don't use the same measuring stick for life as we know it. They measure life in moments, partly because life can be fleeting and, in some cases, the threat of death from war and disease looms large at every turn.

~

Arriving in Nairobi was the easy part. Daniel was already there with Kate, our photographer and soon-to-be dear friend; she had volunteered to document our trip. Armed with a video recorder, we set out on a small, chartered plane for the two-hour flight to Kenya's aforementioned Kakuma refugee camp, close to the Sudanese border. After soaring over a landscape of abandonment, we arrived in an abandoned community. Buckled in his seat, Daniel's fingers grasped the armrest so tightly he could hardly speak. You could see it in his eyes and feel it in his breathing. He was almost home, to be reunited with his mother from whom he'd been separated.

The roar of the twin engines underscored Daniel's quiet jubilation as the dust scattered around the plane's wheels and we landed on the manmade dirt runway. His choice to return was a way of bringing the past closer to the present so he could achieve closure—and keep open his feelings of gratitude, happiness, and love ... or even anger, frustration, and emptiness. You could roll the dice on this one, or—as he preferred at the time—keep your cards close to the chest.

He didn't say much after the engines shut down and hundreds of refugees surrounded the airstrip. He held an expression of amazement as his heart pounded with excitement. I got out of my seat and helped him unbuckle his safety belt. His choice to be here was one of accomplishment. Now it was time to get another set of wheels moving through the dust ... I carried him carefully down the steps and out of the aircraft.

Daniel's wheelchair seemed a chariot to the watchful children and adults encircling the plane. The children at Kakuma were no different than the children outside the airport in Addis Ababa. At Kakuma, they didn't beg for anything; their basic needs were being met. But the children in Ethiopia beg for anything—while they aren't refugees, their hardships are poverty and despair. The humiliation of Ethiopia is mirrored in the eyes of fathers whose own children bring home more money than they can. Despite suffering and privation, there is a sense of dignity among Ethiopians, and they rarely stray from its wellspring.

I wanted to cry out, "Onward and forward!" but the slow pace of wheels stuck in the mud only allowed for a few mumbles under my breath along the lines of, "What the heck am I doing here?

~

We have choices. While some choices are easier to reason with than others—such as what restaurant we plan to visit or what menu item appeals more than another, or the simple choice to be happy—we have the final say. Running away from gunfire is an obvious choice. Starvation, or trying to escape a rapist, is not. The Third World presents a harsh environment for choices, but the positive choices being made there daily—no matter how small—have strengthened a people toward a healthier, more hopeful future.

We can't control the consequences. In relationships and in business, the choices we make determine certain consequences in our daily lives ... but those outcomes aren't always predictable, guaranteed, or in our control. At least, not always in the ways and means we might imagine.

That said, there's a thread of choices that runs through all of us, binding us as one. That's why we must respect and honor the privilege of having choices, and work together toward making choices for the betterment of ourselves, and the world we live in and call home. Of course, we'll continue to make wrong choices, even as we make choices that we believe are the right ones. There is nothing more detrimental to self-worth than doing nothing or staying silent, even if that means choosing the unknown or untried. In the words of Elie Wiesel—political activist, Nobel Laureate, and Holocaust survivor—"Neutrality helps the oppressor, never the victim." Martin Niemöller, a German pastor and anti-Nazi social activist, put it this way:

When the Nazis came for the communists,
I remained silent;
I was not a communist.

When they locked up the social democrats,
I remained silent;
I was not a social democrat.

When they came for the trade unionists,
I did not speak out;
I was not a trade unionist.

When they came for the Jews,
I remained silent;
I wasn't a Jew.

When they came for me,
there was no one left to speak out.

Many of us hesitate to take a stand or make a choice, believing we're safest wherever we happen to be: the comfort zone. This was never more apparent than during the Rwandan genocide when the world hesitated for one hundred long days—with disastrous, inhumane consequences. Many of us believe that the Rwandan people were robbed of choices, as in Sudan's Darfur region ... or in a Sudanese boy who would choose to walk, rather than rely on a wheelchair.

Deprived of empowerment, they can only choose how to respond to their lack of choices, and therein lies the Third World dilemma.

When choices do emerge in developing countries, they generally occur sequentially. First there is dependency—a reliance on others (a handout) for aid and relief. Then, there's a period of preparation (a hand up). The final stage is self-determination and performance, when individuals are empowered to take charge, make decisions and develop solutions.

~

We experience a similar progression in our own lives. For example, we're dependent on others to varying degrees as infants, and throughout our growing up and adult years. As we get older, however, relying on others becomes more of a choice we make. Consider the times you make the effort to call, email, or text someone with no response. Then, out of the blue, at some later date, you hear from them ... either because they just got around to it, or they want something. Never make someone a priority who makes you only an option.

As mentioned previously, preparing for our lives to fully unfold begins when we read the recipe and preheat the oven. Opening our eyes and checking our own temperatures propel us to finally perform as morally enlightened human beings, open to learning from one another.

LESSON 4

Just Add Water –
Simplify Your Life

*"Life is really simple, but we insist on
making it complicated."*
~Confucius

One of the most profound dichotomies our world faces today is represented by those who have access to water, and those who don't. In developed countries, we turn on the faucet and there it is: water, as much as we want. But in the developing world, there's a harsh irony in the culinary maxim *just add water* to simplify a meal. Of all the basic requisites to sustain life, none is more essential than water.

Across the globe, we periodically experience drought in one form or another, usually between periods of abundant rainfall. Here in the West, we might be asked to ration our water usage—which some of us consider an inconvenience. The often dire effects of droughts that plague the Third World, however, far exceed any real or perceived inconvenience.

~

On our first morning in Yetabon, we both awoke early and stumbled into each other on the way out of the doctors' quarters where we were staying. "Sit yourself down and look at that sunrise," Noel insisted. *And a jolly good morning to you, as well*, I thought. All of this, even before I had the opportunity to sample my first Ethiopian egg breakfast. The stillness in the air was punctuated only by an occasional cry from the goats that local villagers kept outside their huts. "We are here to do good, Michael, and I'm glad you are with me," he said. He must have been sincere, because he referred to me by my first name. It was usually "Ditchfield" when I had done something wrong, or if he needed something ... which, I might add, was frequently the case.

"How much more can a man ask than to be able to help in the simplest of ways? We show them a future, not by taking away their lifestyle, but by adding to it. That way they feel we are here to help ... and then they want us the hell out of there," Noel mumbled. It was way too early for his profound, yet disjointed wisdom ... but after a cup of the finest coffee in the world, I understood. We are here to better their circumstances and, in return, they enrich our own life experiences.

The value of having choices lies in simplifying your life. People in different cultures have different interpretations of what it means to "simplify" and make sense of what's around and inside them. You can choose to rid yourself of much of the clutter, distractions, and pain in your life, and focus only on what's important to you, and most valued by you. Many people in Rwanda, for example, have been working on healing by getting rid of regrets and anger. We will not get rid of poverty but we can make the lives of the poor better.

We must first look closely at what is important, and disregard the rest. This allows us to edit life in a brutally honest way, ascribing value to every sentence of our lives. We have a tendency to deliver on others' expectations, instead of pursuing what is really ours to do. This can lead to confusion.

That said, reverse thinking must be taken into account when we are dealing with Third World communities. We should empower what they want for themselves, not what we think they need. This is why asking questions—and really listening—go a long way in providing a hand up. It's really a matter of first getting our own kitchen in order before we knock on anyone else's door.

With simplicity comes freedom, and the balance between essentialism and minimalism. Minimalism is not that you should own nothing—but that nothing should own you. We should all stop thinking about what others think. If we did, freedom would run rampant! Instead, however, the most of our attention is on responsibilities, possessions, and time.

In developing countries, possessions—to our eyes—are extremely sparse. But what they do have, they make the best of. For example, buckets to carry water are rarely traded for better buckets; they are repaired as often as needed. Irrigation channels are the exception, rather than the rule, and villagers in the African communities I visited understand that— until there are enough channels to go around, they will continue to walk hours to get water.

I remember Marta—who I firmly believe is the Mother Teresa of Ethiopia—telling me how she and her family fled Addis Ababa in 1975 because of a Marxist coup. They left just hours before the army arrived to arrest them. They only had time to pack a basket of fruit and chicken before driving an old

Land Rover across 150 miles of desert, traveling by night and hiding behind sand dunes during the day. They had no water ... in desperation, Demeke, Marta's husband, took water from the radiator so his children would not die of thirst. How ironic that Daniel's mother in Sudan also packed a basket of provisions to hide under a tree the night before war broke out. Indeed, the simple means to survive in even the most dire circumstances often mark the beginnings of journeys that forge identities and make us all stronger.

We all have days when we struggle, if not on the level of survival as is still widely the case in Africa, but we struggle with what is tangible to our own lives. Our possessions are usually materialistic in nature, filling a basic psychological need. Whether it's the car we drive, the house we live in, or the clothes we wear, however, there's a tendency—although sometimes unconsciously so—to keep up with the Joneses. The important thing is to offer something of equal value, or close to it, to those less fortunate. This can be accomplished in time ... not just money. As Louise Smith said, "You can't reach for anything new if your hands are still full of yesterday's junk."

Speaking of time, it's what you can and should manage more efficiently to simplify your day. On a much grander scale, the United Nations Millennium

Project offered a "Big Plan" to end world poverty, comprising 449 interventions in all. There wasn't time to address them all, and when immediate attention had to be given to specific problems—for example, identifying how many doses of malaria medication were needed—the other 448 concerns got in the way and very little got accomplished.

I refer to it as having a singleness of purpose. Prioritize your time to work on what the priority is. *Clean your plate of the parsley to get to the marrow.* Similarly, we can't abandon aid to the poor—it's imperative to ensure that it reaches them in a timely manner. As William Easterly put it so profoundly, "Poor people die not only because of the world's indifference to poverty, but also because of ineffective efforts of those who do care."

Rwanda was all about time and responsibilities. One hundred days of genocide could have been prevented, but the United States' recently-challenged peacekeeping operations in Somalia—and a resulting directive outlining a series of factors that must be considered before involving the United States in peacekeeping again—tied our hands. The British, along with the French, were also reluctant to get involved. Only New Zealand stood tall as the lone voice supporting reinforcement.

The clock was ticking from April 6, 1994, after then-President Juvénal Habyarimana's plane was shot down. The world failed to act in a responsible manner, and with every passing day, the stain on the moral obligation to help grew more noticeable. Indeed, former President Bill Clinton and former U.S. Secretary of State Madeline Albright still look at this period as one of regret.

Clinton has cited the failure of the United States government to get involved in the genocide as one of his main foreign policy failings. He said, "I don't think we could have ended the violence, but I think we could have cut it down. And I regret it." It should have been a simple decision to make, but bureaucracy got in the way and responsibility was passed around like a hot potato.

Each of the nearly 1,600 children served by Project Mercy in Ethiopia has a responsibility to themselves and their fellow students during school hours. The nearly 98% graduation rate proves that they take their education seriously—and how they behave outside of the walls of the project shows the even greater reach of accountability. Many of the graduates who go on to a university from Project Mercy want to come back to Yetabon to help simplify and improve the lives of others. They do not abandon their loyalty.

In finding the source of what makes us happy and loyal to our highest good and that of others, we do not have to stray too far from ourselves to find the answers. What water has done for this community in Ethiopia is to help simplify and prioritize the choice for survival and, simultaneously, to reignite hope for a life beyond mere survival. Just as water in this actual example is being put to good use, so can the gifts of happiness and freedom. It begins with looking in the mirror.

Returning to Denver from Ethiopia, the topic of water was on my mind. I made my way to one of my favorite restaurants. I would have referred to it here as a "watering hole"—but, alas, the waiter promptly informed me that Colorado was in a drought and I would have to request a glass of water, rather than assume it would appear. He was only doing his job, and everything is indeed relative, but I felt compelled to share with him the true meaning of drought. My jetlag was his saving grace as I just smiled and said "thank you." I look back on that Saturday evening now, and I realize that the power of those two well-chosen words trumped my initial urge to chastise the waiter, and challenge him on one the world's greatest inequities. Patience, I remind myself. Even grass turns to milk, given time.

*"Wisdom always chooses to do now what it will
be satisfied with later on."*
~Joyce Meyer

How I miss Noel's kitchen. He would always offer a pearl of wisdom that he hoped would penetrate my thick skull. Occasionally, some things got through. I still ponder them every once in a while, although it hurts a little more now.

Once, I asked Noel how he knew when a dish was ready, and whether it contained the right ingredients to make it taste good. He frowned at me, knife in hand (thankfully it was intended for a chicken's neck and not mine), and told me to shut up and listen. (He liked to sound smart; although I'm convinced he was merely smug. It's an Irish thing.)

"The only thing you time in a kitchen is an egg. Everything else is touch, taste, and smell. Don't complicate it, Ditchfield. Keep it simple, stupid." I truly believe he added "stupid" because of me! I would have been fine if he hadn't.

Noel always attempted to simplify things in his kitchen—and in Africa. He was known for giving new servers in his restaurant—Strings—a set of knives, forks, and spoons when they were hired. Curious, I asked, "Why would you go to all that trouble on something as simple as utensils? You have them in the restaurant." "Because," he answered, with that look that goes right through you, "I want it to stay that way. No one is going to steal my bloody silverware for their own apartment." Point taken. I know, however, if they had asked, he would have given them the knives, forks, and spoons ... and thrown in a couple of plates. He was that giving.

~

The Kakuma refugee camp is an oasis of sorts in a barren wasteland—a haven that time is slowly pushing to total abandonment. It serves the purpose of simplifying life for many refugees by providing sanctuary. But in certain contexts, simplifying life can lead to complacency and apathy if the journey doesn't continue on from present concerns. I noticed that daily life for refugees here was made more difficult on purpose, to force them to return to their villages. If you make life too comfortable, they will stay. Of course, the dichotomy is that—even as people are urged to return home—many would be ostracized by their villages because they fled and left the fighting to others.

This decision or impulse to flee is often motivated by fear. And, as we've learned over time, fear is one basic form of human motivation—the other is desire.

Fear has longed raised its ugly head and become a way of life for some. Refugees are given blankets and some food to take with them—these simple necessities will only serve an interim existence, as life on the run can be either a stepping stone or a stumbling block. It all depends on how you look at it. It's not about what the refugees are given to fill a gap and start the journey, but what they make of it along the way ... and what they do with it once they reach a destination.

I believe we must work toward creating a true middle class in Africa, even before all of the refugees have hopefully returned. A class that keeps everyone else honest. A class that has an involved interest in economic growth. A class in which people trust each other. A class that has laws and rules and abides by them. A class that holds its government responsible. Give them a small piece of land and let them work it. It's rudimentary, but it's a start.

We're sometimes embarrassed by the "necessities" we enjoy when we immerse ourselves into the lives of people in emerging nations. Even our own intrinsic needs are brought into question. But, as Noel said to me on our first sunrise in Ethiopia, "We don't need to take away from our own lives; we just need to add to others'."

*"Voluntary simplicity means going fewer places
in one day rather than more, seeing less so I can
see more, doing less so I can do more, acquiring
less so I can have more."*
~John Kabat-Zinn

In Sudan, life was anything but simple. Families were being uprooted, starved, tortured, and arbitrarily detained. Children were tormented and murdered, and hundreds of women endured sexual violence. History has taught us that regimes that persecute their own people rarely confine themselves to killing within their own regions or country. That's why we must, as a moral imperative, look at such savagery and squash it before it becomes a cancer with no foreseeable cure.

~

Daniel had fled to Kakuma to survive; on this return trip, however, it was to reflect. Pushing him past the graves of some of his family members who had perished here was a somber experience for both of us. They had made it across treacherous terrain and survived gunfire, lion and crocodile attacks, disease and starvation ... and after all that, they died from malnutrition, dysentery, and diarrhea.

In Kakuma—at once a sanctuary and a prison—there are bodies in the ground, and bodies walking above ground. Even among the living, souls and spirits seem to have left this place; what appears to be a simple existence belies the ghastly memories that continue to haunt refugees. They are forgetful—their mind plays tricks on them. They talk to themselves and gesture frequently. They even sleepwalk. Domestic disputes take up 90% of the court's time. They burn down neighbors' houses, and inflict pain and violence on each other. They also shoot pool and watch TV together. They hang out and laugh and play board games together. It's the best and worst of times. Meanwhile, back home in America, we keep our mental health concerns on the back burner—even while mental illness is the cause of horrific tragedies on our own soil on a regular basis. We simply can't ignore what is not going away ... whether here at home, or in a distant land.

Daniel and I were back on board the plane as the pilot jumped in to greet us, and to ask if we were ready to head to Lokichogio, or simply Loki—a small town in Northwest Kenya, about twenty miles from the Sudanese border. There we'd find the United Nations, along with more than forty-nine non-governmental organizations (NGOs). Strapped in our seats, the pilot tried to start the plane, but the battery was dead. He'd failed to turn off the power after his previous flight, and now we were left waiting for a battery to be delivered by road from Nairobi. Another night in Kakuma before we could try again.

Driving would have been an option, but bandits ran rampant in the hills on the road to Loki, preying on any vehicle that wasn't an armed convoy. So, common sense won this discussion—although, to be honest, there was no real discussion. A pervasive fear hung on every uttered word. The dead battery was nothing in the giant scheme of things. It certainly trumped a dead body. We would wait.

Upon finally arriving in Loki, we wandered to a local hotel to regroup before our trip to Juba, the capital of South Sudan. The only immediate problem facing me was that I didn't have a visa; I thought you could simply get one at the border. I was told, however, that my passport had to be stamped prior to boarding a UN plane. But I wasn't going to leave Loki and drive through no-man's land to get a visa, and then turn right back around to catch a plane. If I was hesitant about driving from Kakuma to Loki, I was petrified about heading through this neck of the woods.

Daniel calmly told me he would handle it. Of course he would. Or he'd better. The local police officer was a friend of a friend of a friend, probably twice re-moved. He would, for a pre-determined amount of money, take it himself. So let me get this right. I was going to hand over my British passport to a complete stranger for him to go through bandit-infested hills with my likeness in his back pocket? No way was I going to relinquish proof of my identity. Heck, even Daniel was still somewhat of a stranger at that point.

"What other choice do you have?" asked Daniel. *None*, I thought. He told me to simply hand it over to him. It seemed like I was handing over a loaded gun, based on the length of time it took me to release my grip. There is no such thing as simple surgery—the only people who think so are the ones not experienc-ing it. It was the same with my passport. Everyone had told me how simple a process it would be, but they were the ones already holding legal documents. And if the Queen had gotten wind of the fact that I let us both wander aimlessly through these badlands, it would have been the Tower of London for me. To be a nobody in a no-man's land was not on the agenda. Still, I gave Daniel my passport and felt as naked as I had ever been in my life.

The minutes turned into hours as I waited for my heritage to return. In my mind's eye, the "Tower" loomed ever larger ... and then, finally, the policeman appeared with machine gun in hand and passport in pocket. "You didn't have to use that, did you?" I asked. He took out my passport and, as I frantically turned the pages to see whether I was to be accepted into Sudan, he showed me an empty gun shell. "Oh my goodness," I said in a proper English accent. "You didn't." He started to laugh and I joined in, albeit sheepishly and with a much higher pitch to my voice than usual. Such a simple transaction ... *not*.

To this day, I've never gotten a straight answer ... and I'm just fine with that. My visa was there and now I could sleep a little easier again, knowing that I was still a British subject and that my Queen would be there to protect me—along with Daniel, of course, and that rather large uniformed man with the machine gun. "Strength in numbers," I sighed ... and then sleep came over me.

Bring to a Boil –
Exceed Your Expectations

*"The secret isn't counting the beans,
it's growing more beans."*
~Robert Goizueta

I have always been drawn to a short, yet powerful saying by Lou Holtz: "If what you did yesterday seems big, you haven't done anything today." This truth cuts across anything in life where we see the need to excel. It pushes us away from the mediocrity that we find difficult to leave. It comes down to choices again. If you look closely at exceeding expectations or you hear speeches about it, you very often find that this topic is directed toward customer expectations. I have chosen to bypass this area and focus instead on the individual's own personal expectations in life.

Society has a way of turning against two broad categories of people; we dislike successful people, and we dislike the failures, too. "Look at that mansion," we'll say. "Can you imagine the mortgage? They're probably snobs." On the other end of the spectrum, we'll say, "Look at that pan handler ... why doesn't he just get a job?" But we readily accept mediocrity.

Mediocrity is a safe place. Nothing changes because the masses stay as the masses. In England, you are born into a social class and you stay in it. You usually live in the same town, marry your high school or college sweetheart, follow in your father's footsteps in terms of a job, and never really leave that comfort zone.

In the United States, you can rise up the ladder ... but you can just as easily slide down. In the Third World, you find yourself two ladders below, hanging on with every tiny bit of strength you can muster. But don't get mediocrity confused with middle class—as I alluded to earlier, a middle class is what Africa needs to thrive, whereas mediocrity is a limiting state of mind.

"The expectations of life depend upon diligence; the mechanic that would perfect his work must first sharpen his tools."
~Confucius

Daniel and Noel always took the high road when it came to pursuing their dreams. Dreams take you out of your comfortable, predictable environment. A dream is where the road to meeting—even exceeding—your own personal expectations begins.

Daniel insisted on doing things himself. He was a firm believer that individuals are themselves accountable for their actions. Noel, on the other hand, adamantly believed that we can do more through other people's connections (I'm pretty sure he meant "money," but I let him slide on that one). All prominent persons in Colorado reacted the same way when they saw Noel coming: "What does he want now?" Out of sheer obligation, if nothing else, they always came through. You never said "no" to Noel, because you were never sure what the ramifications might be. You said "yes" to get him off your back. But, down deep, you were glad and happy that you did.

I remember one Saturday evening at Strings when former Vice President Al Gore was in having dinner. Noel reached up to the shelf by the front door for Marta's book, *Sheltered by the King*, handed it to him, and commanded him to read it. As if things couldn't get any more awkward, he then told Gore to pass it on to the president when he had finished with it. He walked back toward me as proud as a peacock. "What the heck where you doing?" I asked in amazement. He stopped and got that snarly look on his face. "Listen, Ditchfield, what's the worst thing he can do ... say no?" He had a point.

That point was his hallmark—telling (not asking) people to better the lives of others. And there were many of those moments. I never got the hang of following in his footstep on that one, but then again, I'm not Noel. It was the depth in him that took him to great heights. He was persistent in everything and relentless in everything else. He believed with all his heart that we all must work a little harder to make this world a better place. He always said this while looking down at his watch. Time was the enemy, as well as our friend. We moved quickly when Noel had the starting gun and the stopwatch.

"It is not work that kills men; it is worry.
Work is healthy; you can hardly put more upon
a man than he can bear. Worry is rust upon the
blade. It is not the revolution that destroys
the machinery, but the friction."
~Henry Ward Beecher

I once listened to Noel tell me about boiling a potato. We were in the kitchen at Project Mercy in Ethiopia with the former cook to the late Emperor Haile Selassie. Noel was being Noel. "Any vegetable that grows below the ground is placed in cold water and brought to a boil. Any vegetable that grows above the ground is placed directly into boiling water," he said confidently. I looked over to him and asked, "Why?" He gave me that look again and said, "Because I say so," and then laughed at himself. But he was serious. I still have no idea if there was any truth to his statement, but the Irish are masters at boiling potatoes.

Daniel was happy when we landed in Juba. He was somewhat home because we were on Sudanese soil, but the soil he really wanted to make tracks in was in the village of Panyagor on the Blue Nile.

The airport found me in a barebones security and immigration center—the man viewing my passport wasn't smiling. I'm sure he never turned to the page with my Sudan visa. "No, no, no!" I proudly exclaimed. "Please look at page nine in my passport a little more closely. You don't know the trouble I went through to get that." I then convinced myself to simply remain silent, as now he did look at page nine and then shook his head as if he was confused. *Oh no!* In the words of Mark Twain, "It is better to keep your mouth closed and let people think you are a fool than to open it and remove all doubt." If I felt naked before, then I sure as heck didn't want to get any more "naked" at this stage in our journey.

Swallowing my Adams apple twice, perspiration rolling down my neck, I asked very softly, "Is everything alright?" He pointed down toward the visa. Oh dear, that's Ethiopia, and I know for a fact this is not Addis Ababa. "Sorry, my fault, page twelve is where we should be. I needed to know my numerals a little better." Finally, I was allowed to continue and we all walked onto the tarmac where we waited for our next flight to appear.

I had brought my camera, but why I decided to take it out now, I'll never know. As I happily snapped some photos, an airport security guard hurried over. He gestured that he would take the camera from me if I didn't put it away. Daniel was now giving me the same look that Noel used to give me when he was not pleased. I just couldn't win. This day had to end.

After boarding our flight and stopping briefly in Bor, we finally landed on the smallest landing strip I have ever seen. I was gripping my armrest so tightly that my ring left an impression for two hours. There were many steep, stomach-churning turns—at one moment, I was asking myself why my visa request couldn't have been turned down in the first place? You have to go through what you are going through, to get to where you want to go. Perhaps Churchill had it figured out best when he said, "When you are going through hell, keep going." I was moving as fast as I could.

Daniel was getting excited. This was the first time I had seen him portray that emotion publicly. He was human. He looked over at me and, with little hesitation, he smiled and said, "Michael, you never thought we could do it, did you? See, when you put your mind and wheels to it, you can go anywhere and do anything. Nothing can hold you back, except yourself."

～

Whenever you want to push yourself a little further, either in a wheelchair or with two feet moving one in front of the other, you first need vision. That is what Walt Disney learned after he built Disneyland. There was no room to grow and expand this park after, so when Disneyworld was developed, more land around it was purchased to accommodate Disney's ever-expanding dreams. In rudimentary business terms, this example is often recalled as the difference between a mission statement and a vision statement.

Noel and Daniel aligned themselves to where they should be heading, realizing and accepting that it was okay to make mistakes when you had chosen to take risks. They had a sense of purpose, they trusted themselves, and they grew in the courage of their convictions every day.

Mia Farrow—American actress, fashion model, and activist—exceeded expectations when she directed her vision toward Africa. Here she has worked for human rights, especially children's rights. To show solidarity with the people of Darfur, she began a water-only fast that lasted twelve days—she went that extra mile. In her company were aforementioned "lighthouses" like George Clooney, Don Cheadle, and John Prendergast.

I, too, went on a fast, lasting seven days on the rations given to Kakuma refugees. Even Sir Richard Branson went on a fast on his private island to bring attention to Darfur; I'm not sure how many days he lasted, or what his personal chef found for him to eat or drink in paradise, but I imagine that he exceeded his expectations of himself, too. He could be forgiven, however, if he strayed from the path a little—after all, he was a pioneer and advocate in working to achieve indoor residual spraying of DDT in Africa to combat the spread of malaria. I applaud him for staying the course.

"Fast for Darfur" brought out many other celebrities who also participated for the cause. These individuals went beyond their own comfort zone to raise the bar. They took a stand and made a statement—and the world was reminded that silence helps the perpetrator, never the victim.

"Be kind whenever possible. It is always possible."
~Dalai Lama

As the door to the plane opened, a small gathering of people congregated at the foot of the stairs, each one as excited as the next to tug Daniel's clothing and welcome him home. The elaborate celebration that was to follow was a contradiction in terms to the villagers' usual simple way of life. But it was Daniel coming home.

After a brief jaunt in his wheelchair, shared among different villagers pushing him, we finally got him into a vehicle for the trip to the other side of the village where his mother was anxiously and nervously waiting. The sandy road meandered around areas of land that were under water, but we finally made it to the hut and the landmark tree where Daniel was born.

His mother was the first to greet us, and—with an infectious smile that brought tears to my eyes—she proceeded to give Daniel a hug that seemed to last as long as the second civil war. After she backed away, with one hand still firmly grasped with Daniel's, she began to cry. I looked around at the reaction of the village elders. They were stoic and stone-faced, as if they were holding court. I wasn't sure if it was because Daniel had fled the village, leaving it behind, or because it was simply their manner of being. Either way, Daniel's immediate family put forth more than enough celebration to make up for these party poopers.

My emotions were mixed as I vicariously relished the return of her son, even while it pained me to think of other mothers who had yet to see their own sons, daughters, and husbands return. I got back to the celebration at hand, but was forced into a lesson of self-control as I witnessed the stomach-hurdling event of a calf being sacrificed, just ten feet away. This was a first, and probably a last, for me—but for Daniel and his family, it was an honor, as cattle are highly prized.

Here, Daniel was seen as a leader—he was the center of attention not merely because he had returned, but because he'd been to the United States where he'd gained knowledge that he wanted to share here in Sudan. He had risen beyond what they thought any of them could ever achieve, and he had gone where they never thought they could go.

As we continued to sit around that tree where Daniel and his father were born, the elders slowly began to come out of their shells, albeit with a questioning spirit. One of the more distinguished-looking elders asked, "If America is everything in this world and it can only do good, how is it that Daniel still can't get up out of that wheelchair and walk?" This one took me by surprise. We have the tendency to ponder certain questions by stalling because we don't know the answer, or we're trying to figure it out. I was once told that you don't need to know all of life's answers, because you will not be asked all of life's questions—but this was one question I wish I hadn't been asked.

I was limited in what I knew, but I had conviction therein. I wanted to tell the elder that the Greater Force that put Daniel in a wheelchair did so for a (good) reason—and part of that reason is that Daniel continues to save lives today. Reaching far beyond the confines of his wheelchair, his dedication to helping others speaks volumes of the love and peace he feels within himself. After all, leadership is defined by your actions, not your title. Exploring this principle a bit further, in the *Tao Te Ching*—one of the world's most treasured wisdom teachings—Lao Tzu suggests that it is not so much what a leader gets done, but what gets done on their watch that matters.

The villagers always believed that their loyalty to each other and to their village was paramount if they were to build a better future. They believed in trust and honesty amongst themselves. Being part of a tribe or village similar to these Dinka is an identity more important than having a social security number here in the United States.

Daniel was showing them his hopeful vision for a future—a future fueled by principles of trust, honesty, and love. We all express these principles differently, and that's called culture—the way we choose to meet common human needs. We must strive diligently to acquire an understanding of others' cultures and their peculiarities. If we don't, we'll never appreciate, learn or grow from them.

Math has theorems, religions have commandments, physics has laws, science adheres to scientific methods, medicine has strict standards, and leadership—beyond anything—has principles.

LESSON 6

Simmer, Don't Stir –
Demonstrate Your Patience

"To the forgiving and the forgiven,
may you become the same person."
~anonymous

Of all the lessons in this book, none is more relevant—yet more difficult to achieve—than forgiveness. Forgiveness is one of the more challenging of our values. And of all the countries in Africa that suffered under fear-mongering regimes, none is more accountable to forgiveness and hope than Rwanda.

You can read about the genocide all day long. You can watch numerous films and documentaries about it. You can even listen to survivors talk about it—but you still won't comprehend man's inhumanity to man, woman, and child. It's probably the most heinous one hundred days in history, bearing in mind the difference between war and fighting for freedom, and perpetrating genocide.

Sudan, especially the Darfur area, is still experiencing the atrocities of war and genocide, where the primal urge to simply survive outweighs anything else—even understanding—let alone a spirit of forgiveness that may or may not come. Only time will reveal its hand. So as that clock ticks and we await progress, I returned to Rwanda—a country that offers one of history's greatest examples of forgiveness and reconciliation. And if the Rwandan people can achieve peace—despite their dark, divisive past—then we certainly should, too.

What's remarkable is that they are genuinely forgiving the truly unforgivable. In our lives, when we are confronted with forgiveness, more often than not we're just reasoning with another individual— and forgiveness becomes an arguably sentimental, even romantic act. In Rwanda, however, we're talking about many people forgiving many others for a single monstrous event. As bestselling author and renowned humanitarian Rick Warren put it, "In all my travels, I've never seen a country's population more determined to forgive, and to build and succeed than in Rwanda."

~

On my first trip to Rwanda, the flight from Cape Town finally carried us over the Land of a Thousand Hills. Not very long ago, these same majestic hills and numerous swamps staged one of the greatest massacres in history. You couldn't discern evidence from this viewpoint—high above the banana fronds, and the coffee and vanilla plantations—but, as the days passed, that changed. Said Joseph-Desire, a Hutu killer: "You will never see the source of a genocide. It is buried too deep in grudges, under an accumulation of misunderstandings that we were the last to inherit. We came of age at the worst moment in Rwanda's history: we were taught to obey absolutely, raised in hatred, stuffed with slogans. We are an unfortunate generation."

Making a conscious decision to end the cycle of hatred can be as deliberate as choosing a path of anger and violence—peace can spread the same way acts of violence can. The Rwandan genocide was premeditated. Five months before the mass murder, 987 crates of machetes had arrived in Kigali. Someone, somewhere knew something.

We arrived at Kigali airport to a warm welcome from three orphaned girls and a small contingent of local dignitaries. Upon receiving bouquets of flowers, ceremonial handshakes, and warm hugs, a spirit of acceptance and compassion felt as real as the warm humidity that enveloped us. Even the guards with machine guns mustered up smiles. We were here to bring sports and culture to the children impacted by this dark chapter of history. They were there to teach us about forgiveness and love.

Some have claimed forgiveness as being the ultimate revenge, but that doesn't capture the deeper reason why we seek—and offer—forgiveness. Indeed, a vengeful intent nullifies the act. Compassion runs deep here, now ... but so do the physical, mental, and emotional scars.

As we drove from the airport, we saw men limping with one crutch to support their Achilles tendons, severed by machetes to leave that indelible impression that you carried the blessing and the burden of surviving—and so that others would see and never forget.

Rwandans are traumatized. For some, their distress is current. For others, the impact of the genocide may come ten or twenty years down the road. Trauma disconnects us with life as it's meant to be lived, and affects how we think and feel and engage with the world—as well as with ourselves. Pain causes us to lose trust, but forgiveness helps restore our connection to life and reestablish an inner peace. As Archbishop Desmond Tutu said, "You should never hate yourself for hating others who do terrible things: the depth of your love is shown by the extent of your anger. However, when I talk of forgiveness, I mean the belief that you can come out the other side a better person."

Indeed, forgiveness transcends the prison of victimhood that binds you to your perpetrator. But the process of forgiveness requires the perpetrator to have knowledge of their offense. Moreover, in forgiving, no one is necessarily expected to forget. An evil deed may never be forgivable, but the evildoer can be pardoned.

> *"The weak can never forgive. Forgiveness is the attribute of the strong."*
> ~Mahatma Gandhi

We were here to offer hope to the orphaned children who were now of age to comprehend "what your father did to my family." Instead of picking up machetes, we were here to show them alternatives— they could pick up a soccer ball or a musical instrument, and compete and collaborate in a healthy and safe environment.

Before visiting the different areas around Kigali, I wanted to visit a couple of hospitals in the city. My first stop was King Faisal Hospital, a private hospital, at the request of my dear friend Douglas Jackson, President and CEO of Project C.U.R.E.—an international nonprofit that provides medical supplies and equipment to more than 130 countries. As a Project C.U.R.E. Goodwill Ambassador at the time, ensuring that our shipments had arrived at their destination was paramount (although I think Doug gave me that distinction to get me out of his hair ... and the country). Even so, my business card looked pretty snazzy.

Feeling confident that my work at King Faisal Hospital was complete, and feeling energized from seeing firsthand how good people and organizations can make a difference, I found out later that this hospital was a refuge for hundreds during the genocide. Many had sought a safe haven here ... and many had died here. And then, walking the grounds of Kigali's General Hospital—a place for the masses—I also saw firsthand the remnants of life on a thread.

The HIV ward devastated my spirit. Many had full-blown AIDS. I looked down at two strangers lying head-to-toe in the same bed. Every bed duplicated the one next to it as I walked slowly down an aisle, not knowing what to do or where to turn. Do you smile as a way of offering a moment of reassurance and comfort? I wanted to cry, not only because of what these patients were going through, but because it needn't have come to this. That's part of a larger debate, however, about how—on several levels—the West has failed the Third World.

I left feeling numb and helpless, just as family members arrived for a thirty-minute visit—every one of those minutes expended on sadness and tears. There would be more days like this to follow as I began my education in this classroom of life.

On the second day, we visited the Kigali Genocide Memorial Centre. Only a few weeks before, former President Clinton laid flowers on one of the coffins containing hundreds of bones from many genocide victims. I lay flowers, too, on behalf of athletes of all colors and religions from around the world. It was a moment I will never forget. There are thousands of bodies in the burial area, their names etched on the wall next to the coffins.

The genocide became even more real to me as I scanned all those names. People are often made aware of the number of deaths that occurred, but when you insert the number of perpetrators into the discussion— 50,000 of them—eyes begin to widen. Rwanda is overwhelmingly Christian (56.9% Roman Catholic and 26% Protestant); this genocide pitted tribes against one another, not religions.

Most of us can't imagine being killed in a church, of all places, but it happened. A Catholic church in Ntarama, in the Bugesera district just outside of Kigali, was the site of a massacre of more than 5,000 people. The bodies lay there for ten years ... shoes stacked by the altar, human skulls and femurs piled on shelves. On a purple-and-white banner hanging in the sanctuary is this prophetic statement, "If you knew me and you really knew yourself, you would not have killed me."

Some asked, "Where was God in all this wrong-doing?" Others asked, "Where was man?"

One platform that was key in rousing and inciting Hutus to turn against Tutsis and moderate Hutus was the transistor radio. Free speech—in this case, hate speech—had never been as persuasive as this. The Hutu-controlled radio station prepped its listeners for a genocide the day after then-President Habyari-mana's plane was shot down. (The extremists believed he was going to implement the Arusha Accords, a peace agreement between the Rwandan government and the Rwandan Patriotic Front.)

More than half the population was illiterate, so newspapers had little impact in their reporting of what was really going on—and very few denizens had televisions. Instead, it was the coded message on the radio that was most pervasive: "Do your work. Cut the tall trees." (Translation: "Get your machetes. Kill the Tutsis.") The genocide began that night.

As John Rucyahana, a former Rwandan Anglican bishop, said in his book, *The Bishop of Rwanda: Finding Forgiveness Amidst a Pile of Bones*, "Most of the literate people were already politically aware. While an educated person might question what they read or hear from the media, the uneducated tend to accept it. The uneducated are more easily affected by threats and the emotional trauma that propaganda like this can create."

The genocide was not only limited to Kigali and the surrounding areas. In southern Rwanda, the most devastating single attack occurred at the Murambi Technical School. The school wasn't fully completed at the time of the uprising, when 40,000 Tutsis were persuaded to seek shelter there, believing they would be safe and protected from harm. Instead, after being crammed into classrooms and waiting for days with no water or food or any signs of help, all were massacred by machete-wielding radical Hutus in an ambush over a twelve-hour period on April 21, 1994. In Jean Hatzfeld's, *A Time for Machetes: The Rwandan Genocide – The Killers Speak*, Pancrace, a Hutu, is quoted as saying, "Rule number one was to kill. There was no rule number two. It was an organization without complications. The blade has nothing to say."

The bodies from this ghastly, senseless annihilation were thrown into mass graves, only to be recovered a few years later when they were preserved in lime and placed back in the classrooms. Some victims' arms are outstretched, as if still pleading for life. Open mouths with muted screams are ubiquitous, the mental images of which haunt me to this day. The place remains as it was then, only now it's a memorial site with no pulse or voice.

Imagine being told to hate the person you love! It's one thing to forgive, but how do you move on? Many still hate—not only the perpetrators, but themselves for surviving. And yet, individual Rwandans are now marrying and starting families with no tribal affiliation. If the Tutsis can forgive their oppressors, shouldn't we be able to achieve forgiveness and move on in our own lives?

A wide range of influences affect our willingness to forgive—from professional mediations to family interventions and personal religious beliefs. Rwandans, however, simply ask to be looked in the eyes by their oppressors and asked for forgiveness. As Gaspard, a survivor, put it, "Forgiveness can only begin with repentance. You can't apologize from a distance. Real regrets are said eye to eye, not to statues of God."

We continued to work in Rwanda with the children of the genocide, even visiting with HIV-infected groups. I used soccer as my vehicle to gain the children's trust. When you've been involved in the game at the professional level, as I have, they have incredible respect and admiration for you. The universal language of sports, like music, knows no boundaries, and needs no translation.

As mentioned in Lesson 1, my time on the same field where 200 children were macheted to death was a major breakpoint in my life. It kept me moving forward as I tried to understand how forgiveness was still on the menu after the kitchen was closed. As Kelley Chisholm of Kin Women profoundly observed, "The Rwandan people have not yet forgiven. They are still practicing forgiveness in the hope that one day they really will have found forgiveness."

~

In the most mountainous region of Rwanda lies the SonRise School run by a remarkable individual, Bishop Laurent Mbanda. His vision is to nurture his students to learn from the genocide, forgive the evil intentions and actions, and go on to be upstanding citizens of the world. The school is quite possibly the wellspring of Rwanda's future leaders—some 1,100 students are in attendance, close to half of whom are orphaned. That's a fraction of the nearly 400,000 children in Rwanda orphaned by war, genocide, and AIDS—but it's a start.

Among the inspirational figures who have been instrumental in bringing forgiveness to the fore is Immaculée Ilibagiza. In her book, *Left to Tell: Discovering God Amidst the Rwandan Holocaust*, she describes how she and seven other women were saved by a neighboring priest, who knew her family. He was a Hutu, yet he felt compelled to save all eight of these Tutsis by hiding them in a three-by-four-foot bathroom in his house for ninety-one days. He placed a wardrobe in front of the bathroom door to hide it from the invading Hutus, who searched for two hours. She felt it difficult during their daily ritual of quietly saying the Lord's Prayer to recite the line "forgive them their trespasses."

After finally leaving this tiny prison and sanctuary, she felt called to actually live out what she found difficult to say behind that door. Her mother, father, and two brothers had been killed. Her time in that bathroom led her to seek out her family's killers to unconditionally forgive them.

Some of the perpetrators are still incarcerated. Mpanga prison houses 7,500 inmates—those dressed in cotton-candy pink are still awaiting a decision, whereas those wearing orange have already been sentenced. When prisoners are released and returned to villages, they're given lessons on how to behave and be respectful. The reformed prisoners are taught to be humble and to avoid confrontation—in this fragile peace, we must work together toward forgiveness, to keep the pot from boiling over again.

The difference is not between people who have been wronged, and those who haven't; it's between those who can admit it, and those who can't. I could go on with many more examples of forgiveness, but instead leave with you the words of Alice Mukarurinda on being asked about her story of survival, "If I tell you everything, we will never finish."

LESSON 7

Pass the Butter – Spread Your Love

"To handle yourself, use your head;
to handle others, use your heart."
~Eleanor Roosevelt

Hate is not the enemy of love; fear is. That's why—if we can rid Sudan, Ethiopia, Rwanda, and other hotspots of fear—love can enter in as peace founded on mutual respect, understanding, and compassion for one another. When we spread our intentions—knowingly or not—we are sharing a part of ourselves with others. We're always communicating with words and emotions, or through actions.

I remember when Demeke shared a pearl of wisdom with me that still penetrates my spirit. He was breaking bread when he looked up at me and said in a soft but convincing tone, "The true wealth of a man is not in his own riches, but in the fact he can share his friends with others." That propelled me to continue to offer any help I could to Ethiopia ... not just financially, but by sharing the contacts and connections I'd made over the years.

I continue to invite people that I know to the table—remembering, of course, what Noel always told me, "The worst thing they can say is 'no.'" Some are smarter than me, many are wealthier than me; some show up knowing very little. Regardless, they are all there with the common intent to lend a hand up to those who have no seat at the table.

The greatest achievement for this group of humanitarians will be to have every man, woman, and child in the Third World seated next to them in spirit, so the ones who want to make a difference can. Breaking bread with those who can teach us more than we could ever have imagined; engaging with them in our offices, boardrooms, restaurants—or even at home in our own kitchens—all of us can learn the ingredients necessary to spread the love, so that one day we can all share the same meal. Either I am your teacher, or you are my teacher.

We attempt to share our wisdom and knowledge and—in some instances—wealth to better the world. We do this with the same intent as the Sudanese tribes share their water, wood, land, homes, and even their food. They share what they have very little of, and that is the greatest show of love you will ever find. It's easy to share what you already have in abundance; but sharing what you have very little of is the measuring stick of truly selfless giving.

What we acquire in life goes much further if we make a conscious choice to share without selfishness. When we give unconditionally, we receive unconditionally; but if we give to get something in return, we'll never be fulfilled. Moreover, the power of love should never be confused with the love of power. In African countries, as in other countries around the world, we've come across dictators who certainly didn't adhere to furthering love, instead relying on building their own power hierarchy at the expense of their countries' poor.

～

Jean-Paul Samputu was a mere shadow when I ran into him at the Kigali Arts Center. It was after a dance performance that we were introduced in the dimly-lit parking lot. I really didn't have any idea who he was, and I'm sure he had no idea who I was ... but we exchanged pleasantries about the evening and why I was in Rwanda. After he shed a little light on his musical background, I applauded his passion for his chosen field of endeavor. Little did I know that I would soon be applauding an encore of his compassion and love that resonates throughout the world. ·

Jean-Paul is one of the finest and most accomplished musicians Africa has ever produced, but he is also one of the greatest ambassadors for peace the continent has seen. As a rising star in the East African music scene, Jean-Paul was enjoying life and making a difference. But he ended up spending six months in jail because of his Tutsi affiliation, along with hundreds of others. After his release, he fled to Burundi and Uganda at the urging of his father. He returned to Rwanda after his father was murdered, along with his sister and three brothers. A family friend, Vincent, was the perpetrator in his father's death and went to prison for his actions.

After the murders, Jean-Paul got caught up with the wrong crowd in Kigali, leading to a period of drug and alcohol abuse. In 2002, he returned to Uganda, still filled with hatred and resentment. It was here that he wanted to die; but it was here that he instead found salvation. With the help of a Christian pastor, Jean-Paul found the inner strength to experience peace for the first time, although he wasn't yet ready to forgive.

Still in Uganda, he went to Prayer Mountain. There, he finally found it in his heart to forgive. At the same time, he got a strange and powerful feeling that he would win the Kora, the African equivalent of the Grammy. With these two empowering revelations, he returned to Rwanda to visit Vincent's wife—he wanted to let her know that he was on his way to forgive Vincent, who was still in prison. Even his wife couldn't forgive him ... how could anyone else? She was amazed by Jean-Paul's love and compassion.

But Vincent found it difficult to accept Jean-Paul's forgiveness; he couldn't even forgive himself. Jean-Paul asked Vincent, "Why?" Vincent explained, incomprehensibly, that the "law of genocide" required the person closest to the victim to carry out the murder.

In 2003, Jean-Paul did indeed win the Kora; not only that, he went on to win the World Music International Songwriting Competition in 2006. And in 2007, Samputu was recognized as Ambassador of Peace by the Interreligious and International Federation for World Peace. He later formed Mizero Children of Rwanda, a music and dance group through which genocide-orphaned children engage in music internationally as a means to heal and spread the love. The Mizero Foundation now focuses on teaching gender equality and women's empowerment. Shame shuts us down, but guilt helps us not to repeat history.

Jean-Paul is still spreading the love after all these years. Forgiving the unforgivable was an immense stepping stone toward preaching about how the amazing power of love can help heal the demons in our actions. I am in awe, awakened, and saddened when I listen to the lyrics of "Cherish the Children," Jean-Paul's song of hope that speaks to the importance of positive role models for future generations. Through music and lyrics—renditions of unconditional love—he spreads the love in ways that are comforting to the heart and compelling to the soul.

I found the common thread of love hidden beneath anguish at every destination in every country, and within every group of people I met. I don't have much say in the Third World, but I do have some influence by continuing to spread the love that I experienced on my first trip to Ethiopia. I am now doing what I can with what I have, and with what I've learned.

My decision to go to Sudan to take Daniel home to his mother was to see the smile on both their faces, knowing theirs was an unconditional love—like the love Jean-Paul and Immaculée shared in Rwanda, and as Marta did in Ethiopia. They act out of love because they respect themselves and others. The smile of a mother who has been through so much inspires us to continue to work relentlessly toward eradicating the suffering of all people in developing countries. To do so, we must first think of them and engage with them as equals, truly recognizing their contributions as meaningful and purposeful.

The true leaders in the Third World are responsible people who understand that their actions have consequences. They are generous in all facets of life, giving unselfishly toward the betterment of others, which, of course, comes full circle as they reap the results of their good deeds. They realize the potentially painful and destructive consequences of not supporting the tribes and villagers who are making the most of life with the cards they've been dealt.

Indeed, love allows us to accept differences among all people; after all, the purpose of life is to live; the purpose of living is to give; the purpose of giving is to love. Acting out of respect and compassion—not out of pity—is what's needed universally for all of us to thrive. We are not put on this earth to "save" or change people, or to be changed by others. We are here to love, not to judge.

> *"Love is the absence of judgment."*
> ~Dalai Lama XIV

I remember sitting beside the swimming pool at the Hôtel des Mille Collines, better known to many as the hotel featured in the film, *Hotel Rwanda*. It was a warm, but overcast day. The air was still. The sound of nothing mingled with the pain and fear that had descended on this place before I arrived. The hotel sustained only minor damage in the genocide, but it represented the difference between life and death for more than 1,200 Tutsis and moderate Hutus. The pool became drinking water for the many guests; once the water was gone, it then served the opposite life-sustaining function—a place to hide.

The pool itself had become a sanctuary, as did every room in the hotel. Each room sheltered eight or more individuals; many others decided to take shelter in what could have been a waterless tomb. It was a bleak, eerie moment in history, the knowledge of which still weighs heavily on even an outsider like me. Still now, a surreal mental image appears in my mind's eye when I recall my time at the hotel. Many arms and trade deals, as well as other major business negotiations, have been conducted at this pool—but none of them bear more relevance or significance than the life-saving function of the hotel, and its pool, during the genocide.

But the sanctuary of the pool was short-lived. As the militia slowly moved in, people had to be evacuated to avoid even more killings. The militia was kept at bay for some time, thanks to bribes of cigars, gold, and wine from the hotel cellar. I'm sure that nowhere else in history will you find wine put to such good use as on this occasion.

The humanitarian sommelier who brokered this transaction was hotel manager Paul Rusesabagina, a Hutu who was married to a Tutsi named Tatiana. The murder of the country's president fed into Paul's accurate prediction that murders at the top are usually followed by the slaughter of everyday people. Since he was a political moderate and his wife was a Tutsi, they were both particularly concerned—with good reason.

When Paul heard from a fellow hotel manager that the killings had begun, however, he remained calm. With hurried patience he placed a call to local UN peacekeepers, asking for reinforcement. No help came. He felt exhausted, but he remained in control of his own emotional state. Love for his fellow men, women, and children was the driving force to save them. If he had any anger, he used it positively to take action against the unthinkable.

It's been said that everything happens for us, not to us. Paul showed the world that he was an honest and decent man. After all, if you're dishonest, you're in a relationship with a lie ... and the last thing Paul wanted was to betray the trust of those who looked to him for help. Besides, there were already enough lies to go around.

With outside food deliveries cut off, Paul went underground—so to speak. In the hotel basement, hundreds of airline meals were stored. Sabena Airlines owned the hotel, thereby wielding substantial influence in the rescue effort (albeit unknowingly). Sabena's rosemary chicken with dauphinoise potatoes wasn't just the special of the day; it was the special of a lifetime. What could have been a last meal thankfully turned out to be a taste of what lay ahead—the opportunity to eat again, to be free again, to continue living.

As I glanced up from my coffee, I imagined the fear that must have been mirrored in the eyes of the persecuted here. I kept reliving Vincent's words about the law of genocide being that the one closest to the family or individual to be killed is the one who must commit the murders. It gives a whole different, grisly meaning to the phrase "You always hurt the ones you love."

"Love makes me look at what I can't stand."
~Alice Walker

Paul was drained, but not beaten by the experience. As he reflects on events today, he still can't quite comprehend the volume and velocity of the slayings. He believes it was his compassionate understanding of the Hutus' quest for power—and their fear of diversity—that led him to diffuse his pain by loving his fellowmen. He put the devastation of the genocide into perspective when he looked at the numbers. Some 8,000 lives were lost per day (five per minute); he saved close to four hours' worth of lives in that hotel. Time well spent, indeed.

~

The Great Rift Valley in Ethiopia served as a navigational tool as Noel's and my entourage meandered toward Project Mercy. Passing the scattered huts along the way was idyllic, children waving at every turn. Their ready smiles were contagious, even for the fleeting moment when our Land Rover passed them by.

Upon stopping at one scenic overlook, a hunched, elderly man who was missing most of his teeth walked over to us, smiling—it was a moment I will always remember. I gave him a Jolly Rancher knowing full well that no further damage could be done to those teeth. He looked up with eyes as wide and bright as the noonday sun, maintaining his smiling facial expression as he opened the wrapper. Unspoken love beamed from his face ... if only we could be as joyful when we are given the smallest of gifts.

Only a lottery win might have felt temporarily more gratifying; but when you don't even know what the lottery is, the present moment is gift enough—and the old gentleman sucked on that flavored rock with all the gusto of a kid in a candy store. He even put the wrapper in his pocket as one would a memento. The love I encountered in that moment nourishes me even now.

As we ascended the last hill, we stopped again to take in the view. There it was, this plot of land that offers so much to so many. We quickly got back into our vehicles and started the descent toward the wooden gates of Project Mercy, where healthy, happy children greeted us with song.

The joy on these children's faces echoes throughout the rest of the Project Mercy community. The villages surrounding these fifty-three acres support the opportunity and love that Marta and Demeke have demonstrated to thousands of children over the years—they strongly believe that the Project Mercy approach is the answer to a hopeful future for thousands more children. Project Mercy nurtures love that knows no boundaries or bias to any one religion or belief.

Said Marta, "To fight poverty, you have to attack it from many different directions and then pluck it out. We can't educate children if the only outcome is to make them discontented with the limited job opportunities currently available to them. We can't just treat symptoms of malnutrition in the clinic and not also improve nutrition and agricultural production. We can't teach good hygiene practices if people still need to bathe and drink from the same contaminated water supply. Clean water piped into each home is possible only if economic conditions are improved for the whole community."

Hidden in Marta's every word is the sound of unconditional love, and the message that you, too, can make a difference through love. She's an inexhaustible force of nature who, when asked who'll succeed her when she dies, said with a smile on her face that she has no intention of dying. I, for one, believe that when she does leave this earth someone who has been nourished by her love will step forward from the classrooms she built to lead the next generation. Love is wonderful company when we walk together as one shadow.

LESSON 8

Clean Your Plate –
Finish Your Commitment

*"If you take too long in deciding what to do
with your life, you'll find you've done it."*
~George Bernard Shaw

While children in the developed world may look with anguish at anything green on their dinner plates—purposely delaying the inevitable—they eventually learn to finish what they start (notwithstanding some measure of procrastination and resistance). With sleight of hand, they may slip the green beans beneath the mashed potatoes; or, better still, enhance the nutritional content of the eagerly awaiting family canine.

Regardless, they'll know they've cleaned their plate as requested by a loving and nurturing parent. Perception is reality, and when mom believes you've eaten your greens, we can all get on with our day.

Everybody is happy, especially the well-fed dog. Ultimately, however, we learn that actions do not justify intent.

Put food on the plate of a child in the Third World, and what quickly unfolds is a primal call to action as that child reaches for nothing less than a chance to live another day. The very survival of Third World families is often dependent on the natural environment. They reap the limited harvest they have access to, and make the best of it. They appreciate their food and cherish the manner in which it's served. They do not take things for granted. They also appreciate our help with farming techniques, irrigation, and wells to drink from. And they recognize that—once the recipe is understood and the ingredients are readily available—we Westerners need to get out of the kitchen. We shouldn't outstay our welcome, or loiter by their fire.

We in the developed world are sometimes guilty of throwing things under the rug, hoping that our problems will simply eventually disappear. We do this in business, and in our relationships with others. Too often, we don't challenge what's in front of us, and we lack the courage to complete the task. Sometimes we're more afraid of success than we are of failure. Said Swami Sivananda—spiritual leader, author, and physician, "Self-acceptance comes from meeting life's challenges vigorously. Don't numb yourself to your trials and difficulties, nor build mental walls to exclude pain from your life. You will find peace not by trying to escape your problems, but by confronting them courageously. You will find peace not in denial, but in victory."

Emerging nations will rise to meet their challenges if they are educated and taught leadership values. Marta was given a plot of land and did something with it. Daniel landed in a wheelchair and made something of it. Immaculée was offered a hiding place and progressed from there. Paul ran a hotel and used his function for good. Lieutenant-General Dallaire wore a uniform and used it for good, too. Jean-Paul's gift of music is a healing force. And Noel was given a spatula, with which he transformed lives. We must receive and accept what we're offered in life, and do something with it that benefits the lives of others.

When we simplify our lives and narrow down our choices, we should avoid a place setting for procrastination at the table. We can learn from it, but then we need to run it down the disposal. While it's not the same as laziness, procrastination delays cleaning our plates. We must learn to differentiate between what belongs to today, and what belongs to tomorrow.

Procrastination is also different from postponing something, if the intent to postpone is toward some benefit (i.e., think of postponement as an incubation period). Daniel believed in letting ideas simmer for a while before taking action. Bringing the people of South Sudan together, for example, didn't happen quickly. Daniel continues to work tirelessly to bring the right people to the table, and to get their voices heard. Put another way, taking time for quiet reflection isn't procrastination—unlike the empty promise of "someday," which is as good as never.

"What is deferred is not avoided."
~Sir Thomas More

Slowing down our lives can be therapeutic, even as we perform daily tasks. Rushing through the day is similar to an ice cream headache. When you eat ice cream too quickly, it touches the roof of your mouth, where sensitive nerve endings—stimulated by cold—send a pain signal to your brain. It passes quickly, but it leaves an impression.

Just so, we need to take our time, slow down, and enjoy every passing moment and memory. Even a meal served to a hungry child in a hut in Yetabon isn't rushed. The preparation of the meal, no matter how small, is a source of pride among mothers. Taking the time to get water and sparse ingredients, and then painstakingly gathering wood to build a fire, are part of the ritual.

I visited the cafeteria at Project Mercy and watched over the HIV-positive children in the kitchen where they took their daily breakfast, lunch, and dinner. They mirrored each other in their show of appreciation for the opportunity they're being given here, but death is also on the guest list. As hope, medicine, and nutrition begin to push death a little closer to the end of the table, however, it's an increasingly unwelcome guest.

The feeding center, close to the main gate, is the first sight you see at Project Mercy. Here, mothers and babies fight for their lives. These are the weakest of the weak, but they still serve up a sense of dignity amidst the stench of despair. They attempt to clean their plate, but it's often a slow and drawn-out process, even as milk is brought to the lips of the children. Some of the babies don't survive—having fallen too far below the nutritional measuring stick to be helped, they die in the arms of their mothers. Others, though, respond to the optimism and nurturing of their mothers and the Project Mercy staff ... and 'cheat death, at least this time. But death will likely come knocking again in this part of the world, where it continually tests the very reason the children were put on this earth: to make it better.

Marta and Demeke couldn't ignore the plight of HIV-positive children, abandoned by their families. They built a dorm specifically for them—what was once a cow barn is now a two-story building that the children are proud of, and dignified by. At first, some of the children didn't know how to walk up the stairs to reach the second level; they slowly inched their way up the stairs as if fearing a total collapse.

It takes time to build something, and it takes time to learn how to make the most of it. Marta and Demeke continue to build on what they started.

～

When Daniel and his loved ones had completed the customary rituals associated with a returning family member, he and I—accompanied by the local governor and a swarm of excited villagers—drove to an area about five miles away. Here, the banks of the Blue Nile often overflow, nourishing fertile soil used for crops, especially rice. Dikes had been built to protect some of the huts from flooding. When nature or war raise a fist, however, community members here in Sudan work together to build or repair the dikes during the dry season, which allows them to use the infrastructure of nearby roads to move materials and people.

Here, procrastination is an unattainable luxury. Villagers set their daily agenda to meet their needs, not their wants. Women and girls join in the task of building, not even raising an eyebrow to the hard work before them. The young girls stop by to help after school, if they are fortunate enough to attend a school. The dikes require constant maintenance, but they hold long enough to keep the river back for the time being.

In surveying the land that this community in Panyagor offered to Daniel and myself, I realized just how daunting it would be to build a community center, school, and library here—which had been Daniel's dream and my intention. But I never finished the meal I started that day. Heck, I didn't even raise my knife and fork. I was, as one of the elders pointed out, just another well-intentioned Westerner who wouldn't return. Never was a truer word spoken.

The experience still fills me with shame. I let so many people down. Recalling Don Miguel Ruiz's *Four Agreements*, I had not been impeccable with my word. I could blame it on the developing hostilities of war in Sudan, or on my own procrastination. Everything I had believed in had been put to the test … and no matter the good things I did in other parts of Africa, I failed here to clean my plate.

My word didn't live up to the expectations of Daniel's fellow villagers, or mine—or the expectations I have of others who want to get involved in helping to empower developing countries. I have no one to blame but myself, and there is no one to make amends except me ... and I will. Daniel is still there in Sudan, working to build peace. He has the fortitude and the passion to see his vision through. And therein lies the difference between two people with equally good intentions.

I often walk in the park next to my home in Denver to order my thoughts. It's not procrastination as I'm thinking creatively with a bigger picture in mind. But I've done my fair share of procrastinating—especially when it comes to Sudan. So I'm learning from it, and doing something about it. Eventually, I intend to return and finish what I started. Soon, it will be time to pick up my knife and fork and clean my plate.

~

Walking slowly for two hours each way to get water for your family isn't procrastination, either. The women and children in Africa aren't running errands to prevent starting some other necessary task. In our world, however, running errands inefficiently often hogs our time. The dry cleaners will survive without us for a day or two, and we'll survive without them. There's nothing wrong with wearing a few extra wrinkles in our clothes.

Time is of the essence in the kitchen, and in our lives. A delicate soufflé must be timed to the second in order to rise to perfection. But even an automatic timer can sometimes go awry. Being present in Ethiopia, Rwanda, and Sudan at just the right moment is no different. There are too many plans and agendas, and not enough deadlines. All too often, what should be stepping stones turn into stumbling blocks.

We invent all kinds of excuses not to do something, cultivating creative reasons that block our actually doing something. When others treat us this way, it's frustrating; but when we treat ourselves this way, it stresses our psyches.

We sit there playing with our food for what seems like an eternity, especially if parental eyes are trained on our plates. We sit there procrastinating over whether to assist with the plight of Rwandans post-genocide, or the humanitarian letdown in Darfur, or the impoverished education of girls in Ethiopia. I understand that we can't—and perhaps shouldn't—intervene in every situation. Choices have to be made, but not at the expense of common sense.

Why do we procrastinate some of the most meaningful aspects of our lives? Very often, we believe we don't have all the ingredients to begin—whether in the form of information and knowledge, or resources, energy, inspiration, and so on. Sometimes, too, our expectations are too high, which touches on perfectionism; but we shouldn't allow ourselves to be influenced by potential failure. Whatever your reasons or excuses, there's no cure for procrastination, so it's all the more critical to procrastinate well. Leave the right things undone.

If immediate gratification—so often associated with moving forward—is of primary importance to you, then the cathedral builders of the world would be very disappointed. We email and text for immediate validation; handwritten letters that require time and effort, including putting a stamp on an envelope and dropping it in a mailbox, are becoming a memory; sure, we have to wait longer for a reply—but when we get it, we feel more special, knowing that someone took extra time for us. Small, heart-forward accomplishments and gestures like these pave the way toward accomplishing the bigger things we care about.

Your home looks wonderful after you clean it, especially when you're procrastinating doing something on a grander scale. Or, if cleaning your apartment is the bigger task, then that's what you might be putting off. At issue is our divided self—each of us are two.

What we want to do falls under the heading "making plans," while what we actually end up doing too often falls under the heading "failure to launch." How ironic that this kind of thinking underlies the UN Millennium Project to end world poverty. Very little is getting done because we're too busy making plans (449 of them), instead of activating the most important ones.

~

Immaculée lived out her ninety-one days of captivity with no plan except survival. Lieutenant-General Dallaire didn't have a plan, either ... he just wanted to save as many people as he could, and he finished the job. Marta and Demeke never intended to start Project Mercy ... it just evolved as they started building; they finished one classroom, and moved on to build a hospital. Paul never planned on overbooking the Hôtel des Mille Collines by hundreds of people; he finished the job by finding them all a safe haven with no incidentals tacked on. Jean-Paul composed songs and gave them out freely to remind us what love and forgiveness can do to heal the world. Daniel never had a roadmap or even a road to freedom, but he finished his journey, too.

Even when we're finishing a commitment we've made, we don't need to rush our lives away. Finishing any commitment is a process that sometimes takes a little longer than anticipated. But once we've made the decision to move forward and actually begin, vigilantly maintaining our balance is key, as is continual self-reflection. A meal that is hurried in its preparation is mediocre or spoiled, as is our work in developing countries if we're not intentional and deliberate in how we proceed.

Thoughtful preparation leads to a better understanding of not just the right ingredients, but the best manner in which to blend them together. Rwanda has done just that, as it slowly transforms itself into the "Jewel of Africa." Besides much-needed inclusion of more women in parliament and a more stable economy, the people of this country are healing and thriving at a steady, purposeful rate.

In Ethiopia, too, there are pockets of hope. If the power of duplication was ever called upon to be savored, then taking the individuals and workings of Project Mercy to other areas would be the equivalent of cooking from *The Escoffier Cookbook* and delivering it to the masses. Too many cooks can never spoil the broth when it comes to feeding this world ... many hands instead make light work!

When it comes to global awareness and action, however, Sudan has been on the back burner far too long. Commitments now to finish the course with peace and harmony will be tested time and again. Progress comes only slowly for Daniel and the people of his country—every time he cleans one plate, another course appears. The ebb and flow in different parts of North and South Sudan—and, of course, Darfur— confuses many as to what's working and what's not. And progress is often interrupted and overshadowed by yet another outbreak of hostility. It has to stop.

We must work together to finish the biggest concerns that loom large in developing countries, even while we work alone to conquer our own, smaller commitments to ourselves and others. We must finish what we started, and make time for reflection and learning before another choice is made and our next chapter begins.

DESSERT

LESSON 9

Just Say Thank You – Remember Your Manners

"The roots of all goodness lie in the soil of appreciation for goodness."
~Dalai Lama

One of the most powerful, yet underappreciated terms in our vocabulary is "thank you." It's a neglected term because it challenges our sense of independence and our so-called personal space. Yet most of us are affirmed and supported by the grace of others every day—this realization alone should lead us to more frequently express thanks and gratitude.

We rarely thank even ourselves for taking care of ourselves by going to the grocery store to gather the ingredients we need—and by preparing, serving, and finally enjoying a meal. In restaurants, it's usually the wait staff who receive our thanks— indeed, they are the messengers. But, oh, for the days when we sent our compliments to the chef like a big hearty thank-you wrapped in a napkin!

*"The only people with whom you should try to get
even are those that have helped you."*
~John Southard

The people I encounter in Africa experience gratitude in ways that extend far beyond what most of us in the West could ever contemplate, yet alone fulfill. It comes from their hearts and shines from their eyes with no limits or conditions, only loving motives. You melt when they bow their heads as if preparing their feelings to be perfectly delivered to you. They are genuine and sincere.

While many emerging nations are plagued by negativity, their cultures foster constant offerings of gratitude. They believe in self-worth even while they're beset by self-doubt. They have a reliable support system—tribe members I've met are compassionate toward one another, and they appreciate what they have. Their gratitude implies humility because they understand that others in the village contribute to their own well-being. They are grateful for each other because they believe they are worthy of each other.

Positive experiences are shared among villagers—be it the birth of a child or the harvest of a crop in

Ethiopia. Even tragedy has bonded them, as it brought together huddled families in the swamps around Kigali when death was on the prowl. They were grateful to survive and share their experience with others. Positive experiences of togetherness within can help soothe the pain without.

Project Mercy's high graduation rate is like a big thank-you from the many children who had the passion and drive to finish their education. These children often thank the teachers and staff directly, too, as do the hundreds of patients who frequent the hospital adjacent to the classrooms. Doctors there probably receive more accolades and gratitude than at any other hospital in the world. They themselves take nothing for granted.

Arguably more so in developing countries than in the West, gratitude is founded on the equal-opportunity emotion of friendship. Anyone can experience it and benefit from it. The thankful hearts and eyes of the many people I've met in Africa, and have had the good fortune to bring into my life, are my constant. They may shyly turn from the spoken word and they can't write thank-you letters (although I'm sure they would if they had the means), but their willingness to express thanks is infectious. We have much to learn from it.

~

I have several gifts of appreciation from Africa: a hand-carved wooden peace dove from Rwanda still brings back memories of my efforts to foster peace through sports and dance, as does the bracelet made by the children at Project Mercy. From Panyagor, the smile and tears of a mother reunited with her son are always in my mind's eye, and the simple expression of "thank you" from the headmaster on that soccer field in Kigali still resonates in my heart. Perhaps no thank-you was more meaningful, however, than the one I received from an Ethiopian parking lot attendant on a rainy December evening in downtown Denver.

All these memories cultivated an appreciation of gratitude within me, which I continue to hone and share with others. But don't confuse gratitude with indebtedness—true gratitude frees us from obligation. In Africa, most people I met were equally kind to everyone, expecting nothing in return. Their smiles are a means of being present—not doubting the past, yet looking to the future.

Noel was the only person I ever met who truly understood the sense of empowerment that springs forth from "thank you." He consciously applied it on two levels. First, he used the term sincerely because so many people went out of their way to praise and validate him, dine at his restaurant, or give time or money to his passion for helping those less fortunate;

second, he frequently spoke the term to people who didn't expect it. I, on the other hand, would often stumble and fumble my gratitude in fragmented sentences that left him baffled and agitated. "Just say thank you," he would say. "How difficult is that, Ditchfield?" Indeed.

Noel also had a wonderful way of expressing himself through handwritten notes that he was always proud of. He had struggled in school, and—even though Irish was his first language and his thank-you notes were in English (the way they're supposed to be)—he continued to struggle. He would ask me to proofread many individual letters and notes that were either asking for something, or thanking for something; he even asked me to proofread the letter he sent to former President Clinton. To Noel, everybody was equal; to get rejected by a president was no more damaging than getting rejected by an everyday person. Rejection was rejection no matter how it's delivered, albeit this didn't happen often when Noel was doing the asking. "Well, he just lost out on a thank-you," Noel muttered when he did get turned down. I felt bad for the person who missed out on this sincere show of love from someone who truly knew the meaning of it.

After offering my pearls of critical thinking and correction, he would often grab the piece of paper away quickly and tell me I was full of something.

When I grew weary of it, I told him, "Noel, this is a work of fine penmanship, crafted by a wordsmith the likes of which has not been seen since the poets of Ireland displayed their literary worth." He liked that.

At Strings, I often felt both dazed and enlightened as I watched him greet yet another customer. I smiled a lot in his restaurant (mainly behind his back) because I knew I was in the presence of a man who had no equal. Admittedly, I've encountered wealthier and more powerful individuals than Chef, but none more connected with the common folk, as well as the richest and the poorest people on earth. He helped people bridge the gap between what they were thinking and what they should be doing to help others. For him, Ethiopia was his personal classroom ... and his calling.

〜

Many of us have lost a sense of gratitude for the freedoms we enjoy—whether they lie with the individuals who gave their lives to ensure freedom, or with the opening of a water faucet in our homes. Gratitude brings happiness and optimism if we can stop long enough to equate our feelings with actions. Gratitude reduces anxiety and depression, and helps us sleep more soundly. Gratitude makes us more resilient, and strengthens our personal and professional relationships.

Even more, gratitude promotes forgiveness and compassion as we work to improve ourselves, and to better understand others. Forgiving someone elevates the belief that we are all in need of—and worthy of—giving and receiving forgiveness.

Gratitude spreads quickly among people in the Third World with a lasting effect. Here in the West, we like novelty and a thank-you is quickly forgotten—that's why texting and emails usually contribute little to developing or nurturing meaningful connections with others. Emails get deleted; texts get misunderstood.

In Africa, even messages relayed by drums are somehow more sincere than our quick communiqués, because there's more feeling and forethought behind them. After all, gratitude engages the heart as much as the mind.

The drumming sounds emanating from villages I've visited are individually performed, underscoring the sincerity of the thank-you message. The response, therefore, is also personal. In the villages, someone who can't drum usually has a hearing problem or can't hold a rhythm. In the West, however, if someone can't say "thank you," it's usually because they're too caught up in themselves to hold a genuine conversation with someone else.

Marta and Demeke have been thanking people from all over the world for their money, time, and prayers. They never distinguish one gift from the other—to them, everyone and everything is equal in intention. They recognize that any outward desire to help is governed by individuals' inward passion.

Marta demonstrates genuine gratitude that many would not be able to muster in the hard circumstances she encounters daily. While the couple can't forget the tragedy that led them to where they are today, they still stop to say thank you at every turn. When you look in their eyes, you see peace punctuated by gratitude. The impact of their role-modeling gratitude is evident in the demeanor of the children they serve.

Growing up in the West, good manners are usually taught in some abstract, rudimentary fashion. In developing countries, however, children learn gratitude quickly without much prompting because to them saying thank you for something means that, for the moment, things are better than a mere state of fight or flight. They don't take this lightly.

~

Someone who is offered the grace of forgiveness usually exhibits humility expressed as a thank-you. The emotional punch of this exchange is especially poignant when the wrongdoer asks for forgiveness; and when they've been forgiven, they can't say thank you enough. Jean-Paul forgave Vincent for his father's death—even today, Vincent is continually thanking him for that profound gesture of compassion. Saying thank you never gets old, and it never should.

People who consistently express gratitude tend not to focus on the negatives in life. They focus instead on their blessings, as I've witnessed many times over in Africa. The perceived blessings among Rwandan genocide-survivors prove that—even in the most difficult of times—gratitude will take you further. In a circle of thank-yous that never ends, they count on their families and friends during hardship, even as they reach out to help others. Gratitude heals.

The tribes I've encountered look at the world with joy because they focus on what's before them; in turn, they are less needy or angry than many of us. Like a ritual, their gratitude has taken up residence in their hearts, minds, and souls. Indeed, I've never felt more rejuvenated and energized than when I visited the elders and children of the Dinka tribe in Panyagor.

That said, there was one occasion when the ritual of drumming at 4 a.m. made me question my newfound sense of gratitude (my mood on malaria medication didn't help the situation). I actually yelled out from the door of my hut to "turn those bloody drums down." I quickly returned to the safe confines of my mosquito net. I still smile when I remember that moment, grateful that no one heard me—or I'd have been the last person that the Dinka tribe would want to thank.

> *"Some people grumble that roses have thorns;*
> *I am grateful that thorns have roses."*
> ~Alphonse Karr

The children that accompanied Daniel and me for the duration of our stay in Panyagor were as thankful a bunch of kids as you could find anywhere. The girls carried wood on their heads with smiles as wide as the Blue Nile itself. "Thank you for working with us as we rebuild" was a common refrain in the village. They trusted us.

How many times in our lives do we get the chance to hear the words "thank you" spoken from such a depth of gratitude by people who spend much of their lives hovering on the brink of hell?

I, too, was appreciative and grateful at every turn in the African countries I visited. I count my blessings as if they're priceless jewels, and I never for one moment take for granted the life path I've chosen. It gives me reason to get out of bed with a full heart, because I know that people all over the world are also doing their part to help others. Together, we can stay the course by doing what we can with what we have for those who ask for nothing but the chance to live and thrive with dignity.

~

The next time you hear the siren of an ambulance, fire engine, or police car, realize that someone is in distress and say a quiet thank-you for the helpers among us who are on their way—just as the children of the Third World are grateful to those of us who stand by them in their adversity.

Remember, too, that the thank-yous we *can't* hear are no less meaningful than the ones that do reach our ears. The peaceful silence of a world that could do without war, famine, hatred, rape, and other forms of inhumanity should be wonderfully deafening, indeed. We all walk the same earth—at a different pace and in different directions to different proverbial drummers. Resolve to find your own glorious rhythm.

"If the only prayer you said in your whole life was thank you, that would suffice."
~Meister Eckhart

AFTERWORD

Check, Please

*"Whenever I think of the impact of the Chinese
student standing alone in front of a tank in
Tiananmen Square, I also think of the impact
of an Irishman standing alone in front of a
grill, spatula in hand. He just hasn't had
his picture taken yet."*
~Bill Shore, *The Cathedral Within: Transforming
Your Life by Giving Something Back*

On December 6, 2011, my kitchen was turned upside down. My most cherished pot was missing. My best friend was gone. Noel had decided to take his own life without so much as a goodbye. The last text I ever got from him was "thank you," and the last note he ever wrote to me was a contemplation of "how to go forward." I never got the chance to find out where I was going with him, but apparently he knew where he was going.

My original plan was to complete this book as my own thank-you to Noel. He never knew I was writing it; I wanted to surprise him and make him proud, but I never got the chance. People often ask whether I've reached closure on his death; the way I look at it, I'm still open to his life. I never want closure. I want to feel his presence in every waking moment, and I want to grasp his hand and hear his voice every single day.

At first, I was angry, sad, hurt, confused ... and in denial. There's a hierarchy of emotions we experience when something like this happens; I didn't have a manual to walk me through the stages of grief, but I certainly felt them. How could Noel leave this earth, this way, when we still had new things to do together, and some old things were left undone?

We had started writing a cookbook, and we had plans to make it into a TV show. We had plans to develop our own cookware, too. And we had plans to continue working in Africa. Sometimes, however, the most well thought-out plans never come to fruition.

I took a few steps back after he died. I went into a depressive state and only missed him more with every passing day. The loss of a dear friend is nothing new in this world— I'm not the first, nor will I be the last, to lose a loved one. But each of us responds to loss with varying degrees of sorrow. My sorrow is deep.

Noel reached out to the world, sans discrimination, with love and compassion—and he remained loyal and true to that attitude until the end. He also remained lonely within himself; he fought his own demons behind a facade of pleasantries. His pain and depression grew more noticeable during the last few months of his life. He would confuse being tired with being weary. The oxygenated blood fueled by his humanitarian endeavors was becoming depleted. His frail frame became an abandoned lighthouse whose flame was dwindling.

Noel's final humanitarian act was to extinguish his own anguish. He stood alone and contemplated his next step ... a step into the abyss that would asphyxiate him by the proverbial umbilical cord wrapped around his neck. He released himself of a broken heart.

I often contemplate where he is now and what he is doing. I imagine his first encounter with St. Peter outside the pearly gates of heaven. "Where the heck is St. Patrick? I came all this way, and there's no Irish contingency to greet me." I smile at the thought of St. Patrick hiding behind some heavenly column, shaking at the thought of Noel coming there and running the show ... only now he has to watch his mouth and curb the Irish temper I witnessed in his kitchen here on earth.

There are days when Noel is heavily on my mind; and then there are days I pass through without even a thought of him. It's human nature. But I'm sure that on the days I fail to recognize my friend he is still somehow present with me.

Noel gave freely without seeking personal gain. That's the true meaning of giving ... more importantly, that's the true meaning of life. As Noel asked me in his last handwritten message, "How do we go forward?" each of us must find what that is for ourselves. What we do must be at our own pace, in our own way, and in our own timing.

I can never fill his shoes because the footprints have now vanished, and I am left with the somewhat unenviable task of trying to pick up where he left off. Attempting to walk that first mile in his shoes wasn't easy, but he pointed me in the right direction and he urges me with every step to keep going and never look back. He was my moral compass and the only true north I have ever known. **Thank you, my friend.**

ACKNOWLEDGMENTS

"If you want to go fast, go alone.
If you want to go far, go together."
~African Proverb

It has often been said that a journey of a thousand miles begins with a single step. Of all the sights, tastes, and experiences I have encountered, it's the people along this journey who have inspired me and dared me to dream. Because of them, a vision—and a hopeful future—are unfolding. While I feel honored to call them out here, their influence, encouragement, and worth extend far beyond these pages.

With humility and thanks to my **Kitchen Pantry**, filled with loving ingredients for life: Mum & Dad, Henry Ansbacher, Walter Bahr, Maria Bello, Jan Blankennagel, Hilary Bloom, Michael & Audree Bloom, Corinne Brown, Norm Brownstein, Chris Buri, Kathleen Buzick, Tom Campbell, Norm Clarke, Phyllis Coffman, Mark Cornetta, Tammy Cunningham, Jeff Dean, Daniel Deng, Joe Ellis, Steve Farber, Mia Farrow, Darren Fisk, Craig & Gavin Fleishman,

Janet Fletcher, Mark Frank, Georgia Garnsey, Patrick Gaston, Josh Hanfling, Brent Harl, Gary Held, Chip & Heather Hassan, Rich & Katy Hughes, Swanee Hunt, Shawn Hunter, Bill Husted, Immaculée Ilibagiza, Walter Isenberg, Mo Issa, Chris & Tracy Keiger, Jim Kennedy, Matt Krovitz, Gary Jackson, Mike Landa, Gaylord Layton, Polly Letofsky, Lloyd Lewan, Les & Nancy Lockspeiser, Roy & Esther Lowenstein, Mark Lynn, Brian Maass, Don & Rhonda Macy, Geoff McFarlane, William McReynolds, the Millice family, Ann Motokane, Daniel Murphy, Chris Myers, Jana Rae Olsen, Diane & Sid Papedo, Tom Phyland, Mimi & Keith Pockross, Mike Pasquarella, Amber Phipps, Teresa Porter, John Prendergast, Jody Rein, Bill & Jeannie Ritter, Peter Rossick, Jean Paul Samputu, Sher Sauve, Doug Schmuecker & Julie Stovroff, Barb Scott, Bunny Shulman, Brent Smith, Nanna Smith, Jonathan & Chris Stanger, Tony & Susan Stanger, Ryan Stedeford, Josh Stewart, Alan Strom, Lucy Strupp, Ivan Suvanjieff & Dawn Gifford Engle, Daniel Teitlebaum, Annelise Temple, Bonner Templeton, Alec Tsoucatos, Marilyn Van Derbur, Vance & Jodi Vinterella, Doug Wead, Gareth Weiner, Gail Weingast, Jim White, Tyler Wiard, Young Yang, Lawrence Yee, Winnie Zheng, ... and to the best editors ever, Sabine Kortals and Donna Mazzitelli.

To the **Pots and Pans** always at my side to tackle any recipe, anytime: Paul Bishop, Al Charron, Marta Gabre-Tsadick & Demeke Tekle-Wold, Charlie Huang, Douglas Jackson, Bernie Mullin, Irene Zimmer... and to Noel Cunningham, my favorite pot of all.

ABOUT THE AUTHOR

Author photo by Pamela Mougin

Humanitarian Michael Ditchfield—bestselling author, sought-after speaker, entrepreneur, and former professional athlete, is committed to addressing the humanitarian plight of developing countries.

Ditchfield speaks widely on how to inspire change and promote empowerment among cultures and individuals.

He has worked extensively with children in Africa using sports and culture in furthering the peace process. He remains dedicated to transforming lives by advocating for human dignity across the globe.